The Cambridge Manuals of Science and
Literature

T0352326

CHINA AND THE MANCHUS

A NÜ-CHÊN TARTAR
(14th Century)

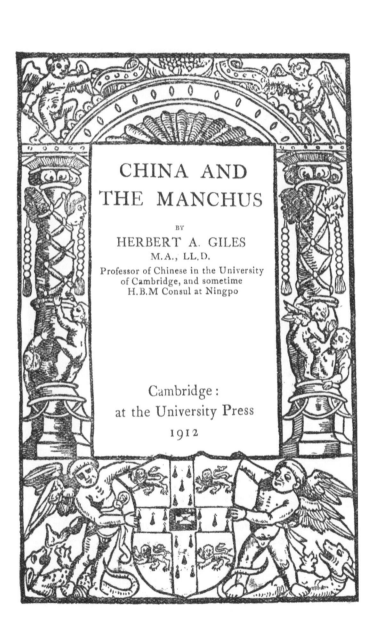

CHINA AND
THE MANCHUS

BY

HERBERT A. GILES
M.A., LL.D.

Professor of Chinese in the University
of Cambridge, and sometime
H.B.M Consul at Ningpo

Cambridge:
at the University Press

1912

CAMBRIDGE UNIVERSITY PRESS
Cambridge, New York, Melbourne, Madrid, Cape Town,
Singapore, São Paulo, Delhi, Tokyo, Mexico City

Cambridge University Press
The Edinburgh Building, Cambridge CB2 8RU, UK

Published in the United States of America by Cambridge University Press, New York

www.cambridge.org
Information on this title: www.cambridge.org/9781107606029

© Cambridge University Press 1912

First published 1912
First paperback edition 2011

A catalogue record for this publication is available from the British Library

ISBN 978-1-107-60602-9 Paperback

Cambridge University Press has no responsibility for the persistence or
accuracy of URLs for external or third-party internet websites referred to in
this publication, and does not guarantee that any content on such websites is,
or will remain, accurate or appropriate.

*With the exception of the coat of arms at
the foot, the design on the title page is a
reproduction of one used by the earliest known
Cambridge printer, John Siberch, 1521*

CONTENTS

ILLUSTRATIONS AND MAP

NOTE

It is impossible to give here a complete key to the pronunciation of Chinese words. For those who wish to pronounce with approximate correctness the proper names in this volume, the following may be a rough guide :—

a	. .	as in alms.
ĕ	. .	„ *u* in fun.
i	. .	„ *ie* in thief.
o	. .	„ *aw* in saw.
u	. .	„ *oo* in soon.
ü	. .	„ *u* in French, or *ü* in German.
ŭ	. .	„ *e* in her.
ai	. .	„ aye (yes).
ao	. .	„ *ow* in cow.
ei	. .	„ *ey* in prey.
ow	. .	„ *o* (not as *ow* in cow).
ch	. .	„ *ch* in church.
chih	.	„ *chu* in church.
hs	. .	„ *sh* (hsiu = sheeoo).
j	. .	„ in French.
ua and *uo*	„	*wa* and *wo*.

The insertion of a rough breathing ' calls for a strong aspirate.

CHINA AND THE MANCHUS

CHAPTER I

THE NÜ-CHÊNS AND KITANS

THE Manchus are descended from a branch of certain wild Tungusic nomads, who were known in the ninth century as the Nü-chêns, a name which has been said to mean "west of the sea." The cradle of their race lay at the base of the Ever-White Mountains, due north of Korea, and was fertilised by the head waters of the Yalu River.

In an illustrated Chinese work of the fourteenth century, of which the Cambridge University Library possesses the only known copy, we read that they reached this spot, originally the home of the Su-shên tribe, as fugitives from Korea ; further, that careless of death and prizing valour only, they carried naked knives about their persons, never parting from them by day or night, and that they were as " poisonous " as wolves or tigers. They also tattooed their faces, and at marriage their mouths. By the close of the ninth century the Nü-chêns had become subject to the neighbouring Kitans, then under the

A   1

rule of the vigorous Kitan chieftain, Opaochi, who, in 907, proclaimed himself Emperor of an independent kingdom with the dynastic title of Liao, said to mean " iron," and who at once entered upon that long course of aggression against China and encroachment upon her territory which was to result in the practical division of the empire between the two powers, with the Yellow River as boundary, K'aifêng as the Chinese capital, and Peking, now for the first time raised to the status of a metropolis, as the Kitan capital. Hitherto, the Kitans had recognised China as their suzerain ; they are first mentioned in Chinese history in A.D. 468, when they sent ambassadors to court, with tribute.

Turning now to China, the famous House of Sung, the early years of which were so full of promise of national prosperity, and which is deservedly associated with one of the two most brilliant periods in Chinese literature, was founded in 960. Korea was then forced, in order to protect herself from the encroachments of China, to accept the hated supremacy of the Kitans ; but being promptly called upon to surrender large tracts of territory, she suddenly entered into an alliance with the Nü-chêns, who were also ready to revolt, and who sent an army to the assistance of their new friends. The Nü-chên and Korean armies, acting in concert, inflicted a severe defeat on the Kitans, and from

A KITAN TARTAR

(14th Century)

this victory may be dated the beginning of the
Nü-chên power. China had indeed already sent an
embassy to the Nü-chêns, suggesting an alliance and
also a combination with Korea, by which means
the aggression of the Kitans might easily be checked ;
but during the eleventh century Korea became
alienated from the Nü-chêns, and even went so
far as to advise China to join with the Kitans in
crushing the Nü-chêns. China, no doubt, would
have been glad to get rid of both of these trouble-
some neighbours, especially the Kitans, who were
gradually filching territory from the empire, and
driving the Chinese out of the southern portion of
the province of Chihli.

For a long period China weakly allowed herself
to be blackmailed by the Kitans, who, in return for
a large money subsidy and valuable supplies of silk,
forwarded a quite insignificant amount of local
produce, which was called " tribute " by the Chinese
court.

Early in the twelfth century, the Kitan monarch
paid a visit to the Sungari River, for the purpose of
fishing, and was duly received by the chiefs of the
Nü-chên tribes in that district. On this occasion
the Kitan Emperor, who had taken perhaps more
liquor than was good for him, ordered the younger
men of the company to get up and dance before him.
This command was ignored by the son of one of the

chiefs, named Akutêng (sometimes, but wrongly, written *Akuta*), and it was suggested to the Emperor that he should devise means for putting out of the way so uncompromising a spirit. No notice, however, was taken of the affair at the moment ; and that night Akutêng, with a band of followers, disappeared from the scene. Making his way eastward, across the Sungari, he started a movement which may be said to have culminated five hundred years later in the conquest of China by the Manchus. In 1114 he began to act on the offensive, and succeeded in inflicting a severe defeat on the Kitans. By 1115 he had so far advanced towards the foundation of an independent kingdom that he actually assumed the title of Emperor. Thus was presented the rare spectacle of three contemporary rulers, each of whom claimed a title which, according to the Chinese theory, could only belong to one. The style he chose for his dynasty was Chin (also read *Kin*), which means " gold," and which some say was intended to mark a superiority over Liao (=iron), that of the Kitans, on the ground that gold is not, like iron, a prey to rust. Others, however, trace the origin of the term to the fact that gold was found in the Nü-chên territory.

A small point which has given rise to some confusion, may fitly be mentioned here. The tribe of Tartars hitherto spoken of as Nü-chêns, and hence-

forth known in history as the " Golden Dynasty,"
in 1035 changed the word *chên* for *chih*, and were
called Nü-chih Tartars. They did this because at
that date the word *chên* was part of the personal
name of the reigning Kitan Emperor, and therefore taboo. The necessity for such change would
of course cease with their emancipation from
Kitan rule, and the old name would be revived ;
it will accordingly be continued in the following
pages.

The victories of Akutêng over the Kitans were
most welcome to the Chinese Emperor, who saw his
late oppressors humbled to the dust by the victorious
Nü-chêns ; and in 1120 a treaty of alliance was
signed by the two powers against the common
enemy. The upshot of this move was that the
Kitans were severely defeated in all directions,
and their chief cities fell into the hands of the Nü-
chêns, who finally succeeded, in 1122, in taking
Peking by assault, the Kitan Emperor having
already sought safety in flight. When, however,
the time came for an equitable settlement of territory
between China and the victorious Nü-chêns, the
Chinese Emperor discovered that the Nü-chêns,
inasmuch as they had done the most of the fighting,
were determined to have the lion's share of the
reward ; in fact, the yoke imposed by the latter
proved if anything more burdensome than that of

the dreaded Kitans. More territory was taken by the Nü-chêns, and even larger levies of money were exacted, while the same old farce of worthless tribute was carried on as before.

In 1123, Akutêng died, and was canonised as the first Emperor of the Chin, or Golden Dynasty. He was succeeded by a brother; and two years later, the last Emperor of the Kitans was captured and relegated to private life, thus bringing the dynasty to an end.

The new Emperor of the Nü-chêns spent the rest of his life in one long struggle with China. In 1126, the Sung capital, the modern K'ai-fêng Fu in Honan, was twice besieged : on the first occasion for thirty-three days, when a heavy ransom was exacted and some territory was ceded; on the second occasion for forty days, when it fell, and was given up to pillage. In 1127, the feeble Chinese Emperor was seized and carried off, and by 1129 the whole of China north of the Yang-tsze was in the hands of the Nü-chêns. The younger brother of the banished Emperor was proclaimed by the Chinese at Nanking, and managed to set up what is known as the southern Sung dynasty ; but the Nü-chêns gave him no rest, driving him first out of Nanking, and then out of Hangchow, where he had once more established a capital. Ultimately, there was a peace of a more or less permanent character, chiefly due to the genius of a notable Chinese general of the day ; and the Nü-chêns had to accept the Yang-tsze as the dividing line between the two powers.

The next seventy years were freely marked by raids, first of one side and then of the other ; but by the close of the twelfth century the Mongols were pressing the Nü-chêns from the north, and the southern Sungs were seizing the opportunity to attack their old enemies from the south. Finally, in 1234, the independence of the Golden Dynasty of Nü-chêns was extinguished by Ogotai, third son of the great Genghis Khan, with the aid of the southern Sungs, who were themselves in turn wiped out by Kublai Khan, the first Mongol Emperor to rule over a united China.

The name of this wandering people, whose territory covers such a huge space on the map, has been variously derived from (1) *moengel*, celestial, (2) *mong*, brave, and (3) *munku*, silver, the last mentioned being favoured by some because of its relation to the iron and golden dynasties of the Kitans and Nü-chêns respectively.

Three centuries and a half must now pass away before entering upon the next act of the Manchu drama. The Nü-chêns had been scotched, but not killed, by their Mongol conquerors, who, one hundred and thirty-four years later (1368), were themselves driven out of China, a pure native dynasty being

re-established under the style of Ming, " Bright."
During the ensuing two hundred years the Nü-chêns
were scarcely heard of, the House of Ming being
busily occupied in other directions. Their warlike
spirit, however, found scope and nourishment in the
expeditions organised against Japan and Tan-lo,
or Quelpart, as named by the Dutch, a large island
to the south of the Korean peninsula ; while on the
other hand the various tribes scattered over a portion
of the territory known to Europeans as Manchuria,
availed themselves of long immunity from attack
by the Chinese to advance in civilization and prosperity. It may be noted here that " Manchuria"
is unknown to the Chinese or to the Manchus themselves as a geographical expression. The present
extensive home of the Manchus is usually spoken of
as the Three Eastern Provinces, namely, (1) Shêng-
king, or Liao-tung, or Kuan-tung, (2) Kirin, and
(3) Heilungchiang or Tsitsihar.

Among the numerous small independent com-
munities above mentioned, which traced their
ancestry to the Nü-chêns of old, one of the smallest,
the members of which inhabited a tract of territory
due east of what is now the city of Mukden, and were
shortly to call themselves Manchus,—the origin of
the name is not known,—produced, in 1559, a young
hero who altered the course of Chinese history to
such an extent that for nearly three hundred years

his descendants sat on the throne of China, and ruled over what was for a great portion of the time the largest empire on earth. Nurhachu, the real founder of the Manchu power, was born in 1559, from a virile stock, and was soon recognised to be an extraordinary child. We need not linger over his dragon face, his phœnix eye, or even over his large, drooping ears, which have always been associated by the Chinese with intellectual ability. He first came into prominence in 1583, when, at twenty-four years of age, he took up arms, at the head of only one hundred and thirty men, in connection with the treacherous murder by a rival chieftain of his father and grandfather, who had ruled over a petty principality of almost infinitesimal extent ; and he finally succeeded three years later in securing from the Chinese, who had been arrayed against him, not only the surrender of the murderer, but also a sum of money and some robes of honour. He was further successful in negotiating a treaty, under the terms of which Manchu furs could be exchanged at certain points for such Chinese commodities as cotton, sugar, and grain.

In 1587, Nurhachu buil a walled city, and established an administration in his tiny principality, the even-handed justice and purity of which soon attracted a large number of settlers, and before very long he had succeeded in amalgamating five Manchu

States under his personal rule. Extension of territory by annexation after victories over neighbouring States followed as a matter of course, the result being that his growing power came to be regarded with suspicion, and even dread. At length, a joint attempt on the part of seven States, aided by two Mongol chieftains, was made to crush him ; but, although numerical superiority was overpoweringly against him, he managed to turn the enemy's attack into a rout, killed four thousand men, and captured three thousand horses, besides other booty. Following up this victory by further annexations, he now began to present a bold front to the Chinese, declaring himself independent, and refusing any longer to pay tribute. In 1603, he built himself a new capital, Hingking, which he placed not very far east of the modern Mukden, and there he received envoys from the Mongolian chieftains, sent to congratulate him on his triumph.

At this period the Manchus, whose spoken words were polysyllabic, and not monosyllabic like Chinese, had no written language beyond certain rude attempts at alphabetic writing, formed from Chinese characters, and found to be of little practical value. The necessity for something more convenient soon appealed to the prescient and active mind of Nurhachu ; accordingly, in 1599, he gave orders to two learned scholars to prepare a suitable script for his rapidly increasing subjects. This they accomplished by basing the new script upon Mongol, which had been invented in 1269, by Baschpa, or 'Phagspa, a Tibetan lama, acting under the direction of Kublai Khan. Baschpa had based his script upon the written language of the Ouigours, who were descendants of the Hsiung-nu, or Huns. The Ouigours, known by that name since the year 629, were once the ruling race in the regions which now form the khanates of Khiva and Bokhara, and had been the first of the tribes of Central Asia to have a script of their own. This they formed from the Estrangelo Syriac of the Nestorians, who appeared in China in the early part of the seventh century. The Manchu written language, therefore, is lineally descended from Syriac ; indeed, the family likeness of both Manchu and Mongol to the parent stem is quite obvious, except that these two scripts, evidently influenced by Chinese, are written vertically, though, unlike Chinese, they are read from left to right. Thirty-three years later various improvements were introduced, leaving the Manchu script precisely as we find it at the present day.

In 1613, Nurhachu had gathered about him an army of some forty thousand men ; and by a series of raids in various directions, he further gradually succeeded in extending considerably the boundaries of his kingdom. There now remained but one large and important State, towards the annexation of which he directed all his efforts. After elaborate preparations which extended over more than two years, at the beginning of which (1616) the term Manchu (etymology unknown) was definitively adopted as a national title, Nurhachu, in 1618, drew up a list of grievances against the Chinese, under which he declared that his people had been and were still suffering, and solemnly committed it to the flames,—a recognised method of communication with the spirits of heaven and earth. This document consisted of seven clauses, and was addressed to the Emperor of China ; it was, in fact, a declaration of war. The Chinese, who were fast becoming aware that a dangerous enemy had arisen, and that their own territory would be the next to be threatened, at length decided to oppose any further progress on the part of Nurhachu ; and with this view dispatched an army of two hundred thousand men against him. These troops, many of whom were physically unfit, were divided on arrival at Mukden into four bodies, each with some separate aim, the achievement of which was to conduce to the speedy disruption of Nurhachu's power. The issue of this move was certainly not expected on either side. In a word, Nurhachu defeated his Chinese antagonists in detail, finally inflicting such a crushing blow that he was left completely master of the situation, and before very long had realised the chief object of his ambition, namely, the reunion under one rule of those states into which the Golden Dynasty had been broken up when it collapsed before the Mongols in 1234.

CHAPTER II

IT is almost a conventionalism to attribute the fall of a Chinese dynasty to the malign influence of eunuchs. The Imperial court was undoubtedly at this date entirely in the hands of eunuchs, who occupied all kinds of lucrative posts for which they were quite unfitted, and even accompanied the army, nominally as officials, but really as spies upon the generals in command. One of the most notorious of these was Wei Chung-hsien, whose career may be taken as typical of his class. He was a native of Su-ning in Chihli, of profligate character, who made himself a eunuch, and changed his name to Li Chin-chung. Entering the palace, he managed by bribery to get into the service of the mother of the future Emperor, posthumously canonised as Hsi Tsung, and became the paramour of that weak monarch's wet-nurse. The pair gained the Emperor's affection to an extraordinary degree, and Wei, an ignorant brute, was the real ruler of China during the reign of Hsi Tsung. He always took care to present memorials and other State papers when his Majesty was engrossed in carpentry,

14

and the Emperor would pretend to know all about
the question, and tell Wei to deal with it. Aided
by unworthy censors, a body of officials who are
supposed to be the " eyes and ears " of the monarch,
and privileged to censure him for misgovernment,
he gradually drove all loyal men from office, and
put his opponents to cruel and ignominious deaths.
He persuaded Hsi Tsung to enrol a division of eunuch
troops, ten thousand strong, armed with muskets ;
while, by causing the Empress to have a mis-
carriage, his paramour cleared his way to the throne.
Many officials espoused his cause, and the infatuated
sovereign never wearied of loading him with favours.
In 1626, temples were erected to him in all the provinces except Fuhkien, his image received Imperial
honours, and he was styled Nine Thousand Years,
i.e. only one thousand less than the Emperor
himself, the Chinese term in the latter case being
wan sui, which has been adopted by the Japanese
as *banzai*. All successes were ascribed to his influence, a Grand Secretary declaring that his virtue
had actually caused the appearance of a " unicorn "
in Shantung. In 1627, he was likened in a memorial
to Confucius, and it was decreed that he should be
worshipped with the Sage in the Imperial Academy.
His hopes were overthrown by the death of Hsi
Tsung, whose successor promptly dismissed him.
He hanged himself to escape trial, and his corpse

was disembowelled. His paramour was executed, and in 1629, nearly three hundred persons were convicted and sentenced to varying penalties for being connected with his schemes.

Jobbery and corruption were rife ; and at the present juncture these agencies were successfully employed to effect the recall of a really able general who had been sent from Peking to recover lost ground, and prevent further encroachments by the Manchus. For a time, Nurhachu had been held in check by his skilful dispositions of troops, Mukden was strongly fortified, and confidence generally was restored ; but the fatal policy of the new general rapidly alienated the Chinese inhabitants, and caused them to enter secretly into communication with the Manchus. It was thus that in 1621 Nurhachu was in a position to advance upon Mukden. Encamping within a mile or two of the city, he sent forward a reconnoitring party, which was immediately attacked by the Chinese commandant at the head of a large force. The former fled, and the latter pursued, only to fall into the inevitable ambush ; and the Chinese troops, on retiring in their turn, found that the bridge across the moat had been destroyed by traitors in their own camp, so that they were unable to re-enter the city. Thus Mukden fell, the prelude to a series of further victories, one of which was the rout of an army sent to retake Mukden, and the chief of which was the capture of Liao-yang, now remembered in connection with the Russo-Japanese war. In many of these engagements the Manchus, whose chief weapon was the long bow, which they used with deadly effect, found themselves opposed by artillery, the use of which had been taught to the Chinese by Adam Schaal, the Jesuit father. The supply of powder, however, had a way of running short, and at once the pronounced superiority of the Manchu archers prevailed.

Other cities now began to tender a voluntary submission, and many Chinese took to shaving the head and wearing the queue, in acknowledgment of their allegiance to the Manchus. All, however, was not yet over, for the growing Manchu power was still subjected to frequent attacks from Chinese arms in directions as far as possible removed from points where Manchu troops were concentrated. Meanwhile Nurhachu gradually extended his borders eastward, until in 1625, the year in which he placed his capital at Mukden, his frontiers reached to the sea on the east and to the river Amur on the north, the important city of Ning-yüan being almost the only possession remaining to the Chinese beyond the Great Wall. The explanation of this is as follows.

An incompetent general, as above mentioned, had been sent at the instance of the eunuchs to supersede

B

an officer who had been holding his own with considerable success, but who was not a *persona grata* at court. The new general at once decided that no territory outside the Great Wall was to be held against the Manchus, and gave orders for the immediate retirement of all troops and Chinese residents generally. To this command the civil governor of Ning-yüan, and the military commandant, sent an indignant protest, writing out an oath with their blood that they would never surrender the city. Nurhachu seized the opportunity, and delivered a violent attack, with which he seemed to be making some progress, until at length artillery was brought into play. The havoc caused by guns at close quarters was terrific, and the Manchus fled. This defeat was a blow from which Nurhachu never recovered; his chagrin brought on a serious illness, and he died in 1626, aged sixty-eight. Later on, when his descendants were sitting upon the throne of China, he was canonised as T'ai Tsu, the Great Ancestor, the representatives of the four preceding generations of his family being canonised as Princes.

Nurhachu was succeeded by his fourth son, Abkhai, then thirty-four years of age, and a tried warrior. His reign began with a correspondence between himself and the governor who had been the successful defender of Ning-yüan, in which some attempt was made to conclude a treaty of peace.

The Chinese on their side demanded the return of all captured cities and territory ; while the Manchus, who refused to consider any such terms, suggested that China should pay them a huge subsidy in money, silk, etc., in return for which they offered but a moderate supply of furs, and something over half a ton of ginseng (*Panax repens*), the famous forked root said to resemble the human body, and much valued by the Chinese as a strengthening medicine. This, of course, was a case of " giving too little and asking too much," and the negotiations came to nothing. In 1629, Abkhai, who by this time was master of Korea, marched upon Peking, at the head of a large army, and encamped within a few miles from its walls ; but he was unable to capture the city, and had finally to retire. The next few years were devoted by the Manchus, who now began to possess artillery of their own casting, to the conquest of Mongolia, in the hope of thus securing an easy passage for their armies into China. An offer of peace was now made by the Chinese Emperor, for reasons shortly to be stated ; but the Manchu terms were too severe, and hostilities were resumed, the Manchus chiefly occupying themselves in devastating the country round Peking, their numbers being constantly swelled by a stream of deserters from the Chinese ranks. In 1643, Abkhai died ; he was succeeded by his ninth son, a boy of five, and was later on canonised as T'ai Tsung, the Great Fore-father. By 1635, he had already begun to style himself Emperor of China, and had established a system of public examinations. The name of the dynasty had been "Manchu" ever since 1616; twenty years later he translated this term into the Chinese word *Ch'ing* (or Ts'ing), which means "pure"; and as the Great Pure Dynasty it will be remembered in history. Other important enactments of his reign were prohibitions against the use of tobacco, which had been recently introduced into Manchuria from Japan, through Korea; against the Chinese fashion of dress and of wearing the hair; and against the practice of binding the feet of girls. All except the first of these were directed towards the complete denationalisation of the Chinese who had accepted his rule, and whose numbers were increasing daily.

So far, the Manchus seem to have been little influenced by religious beliefs or scruples, except of a very primitive kind; but when they came into closer contact with the Chinese, Buddhism began to spread its charms, and not in vain, though strongly opposed by Abkhai himself.

By 1635 the Manchus had effected the conquest of Mongolia, aided to a great extent by frequent defections of large bodies of Mongols who had been exasperated by their own ill-treatment at the hands of the Chinese. Among some ancient Mongolian archives there has recently been discovered a document, dated 1636, under which the Mongol chiefs recognised the suzerainty of the Manchu Emperor. It was, however, stipulated that, in the event of the fall of the dynasty, all the laws existing previously to this date should again come into force.

A brief review of Chinese history during the later years of Manchu progress, as described above, discloses a state of things such as will always be found to prevail towards the close of an outworn dynasty. Almost from the day when, in 1628, the last Emperor of the Ming Dynasty ascended the throne, national grievances began to pass from a simmering and more or less latent condition to a state of open and acute hostility.   The exactions and tyranny of the eunuchs had led to increased taxation and general discontent ; and the horrors of famine now enhanced the gravity of the situation.   Local outbreaks were common, and were with difficulty suppressed.   The most capable among Chinese generals of the period, Wu San-kuei, shortly to play a leading part in the dynastic drama, was far away, employed in resisting the invasions of the Manchus, when a very serious rebellion, which had been in preparation for some years, at length burst violently forth.

Li Tzŭ-ch'êng was a native of Shensi, who, before he was twenty years old, had succeeded his father as village beadle. The famine of 1627 had brought him into trouble over the land-tax, and in 1629 he turned brigand, but without conspicuous success during the following ten years. In 1640, he headed a small gang of desperadoes, and overrunning parts of Hupeh and Honan, was soon in command of a large army. He was joined by a female bandit, formerly a courtesan, who advised him to avoid slaughter and to try to win the hearts of the people. In 1642, after several attempts to capture the city of K'ai-fêng, during one of which his left eye was destroyed by an arrow, he at length succeeded, chiefly in consequence of a sudden rise of the Yellow River, the waters of which rushed through a canal originally intended to fill the city moat and flood out the rebels. The rise of the river, however, was so rapid and so unusually high that the city itself was flooded, and an enormous number of the inhabitants perished, the rest seeking safety in flight to higher ground.

By 1644, Li Tzǔ-ch'êng had reduced the whole of the province of Shensi; whereupon he began to advance on Peking, proclaiming himself first Emperor of the Great Shun Dynasty, the term *shun* implying harmony between rulers and ruled. Terror reigned at the Chinese court, especially as meteorological and other portents appeared in unusually large numbers, as though to justify the panic. The

Emperor was in despair ; the exchequer was empty, and there was no money to pay the troops, who, in any case, were too few to man the city walls. Each of the Ministers of State was anxious only to secure his own safety. Li Tzŭ-ch'êng's advance was scarcely opposed, the eunuch commanders of cities and passes hastening to surrender them and save their own lives. For, in case of immediate surrender, no injury was done by Li to life or property, and even after a short resistance only a few lives were exacted as penalty ; but a more obstinate defence was punished by burning and looting and universal slaughter.

The Emperor was now advised to send for Wu San-kuei ; but that step meant the end of further resistance to the invading Manchus on the east, and for some time he would not consent. Meanwhile, he issued an Imperial proclamation, such as is usual on these occasions, announcing that all the troubles which had come upon the empire were due to his own incompetence and unworthiness, as confirmed by the droughts, famines, and other signs of divine wrath, of recent occurrence ; that the administration was to be reformed, and only virtuous and capable officials would be employed. The near approach, however, of Li's army at length caused the Emperor to realise that it was Wu San-kuei or nothing, and belated messengers were dispatched

to summon him to the defence of the capital.   Long
before he could possibly arrive, a gate of the southern
city of Peking was treacherously opened by the
eunuch in charge of it, and the next thing the
Emperor saw was his capital in flames.   He then
summoned the Empress and the court ladies, and
bade them each provide for her own safety.   He
sent his three sons into hiding, and actually killed
with his own hand several of his favourites, rather
than let them fall into the hands of the One-Eyed
Rebel.   He attempted the same by his daughter,
a young girl, covering his face with the sleeve of his
robe ; but in his agony of mind he failed in his blow,
and only succeeded in cutting off an arm, leaving the
unfortunate princess to be dispatched later on by the
Empress.   After this, in concert with a trusted
eunuch and a few attendants, he disguised himself,
and made an attempt to escape from the city by
night ; but they found the gates closed, and the
guard refused to allow them to pass.   Returning to
the palace in the early morning, the Emperor caused
the great bell to be rung as usual to summon the
officers of government to audience ; but no one
came.   He then retired, with his faithful eunuch,
to a kiosque, on what is known as the Coal Hill, in
the palace grounds, and there wrote a last decree on
the lapel of his coat :—" I, poor in virtue and of
contemptible personality, have incurred the wrath

of God on high. My Ministers have deceived me.
I am ashamed to meet my ancestors ; and therefore
I myself take off my crown, and with my hair
covering my face, await dismemberment at the hands
of the rebels. Do not hurt a single one of my
people ! " Emperor and eunuch then committed
suicide by hanging themselves, and the Great Ming
Dynasty was brought to an end.

Li Tzŭ-ch'êng made a grand official entry into
Peking, upon which many of the palace ladies committed suicide. The bodies of the two Empresses
were discovered, and the late Emperor's sons were
captured and kindly treated ; but of the Emperor
himself there was for some time no trace. At length
his body was found, and was encoffined, together
with those of the Empresses, by order of Li Tzŭ-
ch'êng, by-and-by to receive fit and proper burial
at the hands of the Manchus.

Li Tzŭ-ch'êng further possessed himself of the
persons of Wu San-kuei's father and affianced bride,
the latter of whom, a very beautiful girl, he intended
to keep for himself. He next sent off a letter to Wu
San-kuei, offering an alliance against the Manchus,
which was fortified by another letter from Wu San-
kuei's father, urging his son to fall in with Li's
wishes, especially as his own life would be dependent
upon the success of the mission. Wu San-kuei had
already started on his way to relieve the capital

when he heard of the events above recorded; and it seems probable that he would have yielded to circumstances and persuasion but for the fact that Li had seized the girl he intended to marry. This decided him; he retraced his steps, shaved his head after the required style, and joined the Manchus.

It was not very long before Li Tzŭ-ch'êng's army was in full pursuit, with the twofold object of destroying Wu San-kuei and recovering Chinese territory already occupied by the Manchus. In the battle which ensued, all these hopes were dashed; Li sustained a crushing defeat, and fled to Peking. There he put to death the Ming princes who were in his hands, and completely exterminated Wu San-kuei's family, with the exception of the girl above mentioned, whom he carried off after having looted and burnt the palace and other public buildings. Now was the opportunity of the Manchus; and with the connivance and loyal aid of Wu San-kuei, the Great Ch'ing Dynasty was established.

Li Tzŭ-ch'êng, who had officially mounted the Dragon Throne as Emperor of China nine days after his capture of Peking, was now hotly pursued by Wu San-kuei, who had the good fortune to recover from the rebels the girl, who had been taken with them in their flight, and whom he then married. Li Tzŭ-ch'êng retreated westwards; and after two vain attempts to check the pursuers, his army began to melt away. Driven south, he held Wu-ch'ang for a time; but ultimately he fled down the Yang-tsze, and was slain by local militia in Hupeh.

Li was a born soldier. Even hostile writers admit that his army was wonderfully well disciplined, and that he put a stop to the hideous atrocities which had made his name a terror in the empire, just so soon as he found that he could accomplish his ends by milder means. His men were obliged to march light, very little baggage being allowed; his horses were most carefully looked after. He himself was by nature calm and cold, and his manner of life was frugal and abstemious.

CHAPTER III

THE back of the rebellion was now broken ; but an alien race, called in to drive out the rebels, found themselves in command of the situation. Wu San-kuei had therefore no alternative but to acknowledge the Manchus definitively as the new rulers of China, and to obtain the best possible terms for his country. Ever since the defeat of Li by the combined forces of Chinese and Manchus, it had been perfectly well understood that the latter were to be supported in their bid for Imperial power, and the conditions under which the throne was to be transferred were as follows :—(1) No Chinese women were to be taken into the Imperial seraglio ; (2) the Senior Classic at the great triennial examination, on the results of which successful candidates were drafted into the public service, was never to be a Manchu ; (3) Chinese men were to adopt the Manchu dress, shaving the front part of the head and plaiting the back hair into a queue, but they were to be allowed burial in the costume of the Mings ; (4) Chinese women were not to adopt the Manchu dress, nor to cease to

compress their feet, in accordance with ancient
custom.

Wu San-kuei was loaded with honours, among
others with a triple-eyed peacock's feather, a decora-
tion introduced, together with the " button " at the
top of the hat, by the Manchus, and classed as single-,
double-, and triple-eyed, according to merit.   A few
years later, his son married the sister of the Emperor ;
and a few years later still, he was appointed one of
three feudatory princes, his rule extending over the
huge provinces of Yünnan and Ssŭch'uan.   There
we shall meet him again.

The new Emperor, the ninth son of Abkhai, best
known by his year-title as Shun Chih (favourable
sway), was a child of seven when he was placed upon
the throne in 1644, under the regency of an uncle ;
and by the time he was twelve years old, the uncle
had died, leaving him to his own resources.   Before
his early death, the regent had already done some
excellent work on behalf of his nephew.   He had
curtailed the privileges of the eunuchs to such an
extent that for a hundred and fifty years to come,—so
long, in fact, as the empire was in the hands of wise
rulers,—their malign influence was inappreciable in
court circles and politics generally.   He left Chinese
officials in control of the civil administration,
keeping closely to the lines of the system which had
obtained under the previous dynasty ; he did not

hastily press for the universal adoption of Manchu
costume ; and he even caused sacrificial ceremonies
to be performed at the mausolea of the Ming
Emperors.   One new rule of considerable importance
seems to have been introduced by the Manchus,
namely, that no official should be allowed to hold
office within the boundaries of his own province.
Ostensibly a check on corrupt practices, it is probable that this rule had a more far-reaching political
purport.   The members of the Han-lin College
presented an address praying him (1) to prepare a list
of all worthy men ; (2) to search out such of these
as might be in hiding ; (3) to exterminate all rebels ;
(4) to proclaim an amnesty ; (5) to establish peace ;
(6) to disband the army, and (7) to punish corrupt
officials.

The advice conveyed in the second clause of the
above was speedily acted upon, and a number of
capable men were secured for the government service.
At the same time, with a view to the full technical
establishment of the dynasty, the Imperial ancestors
were canonised, and an ancestral shrine was duly
constituted.   The general outlook would now appear
to have been satisfactory from the point of view of
Manchu interests ; but from lack of means of communication, China had in those days almost the con-
notation of space infinite, and events of the highest
importance, involving nothing less than the change

of a dynasty, could be carried through in one portion
of the empire before their imminence had been more
than whispered in another. No sooner was Peking
taken by the One-Eyed Rebel, than a number of
officials fled southwards and took refuge in Nanking,
where they set up a grandson of the last Emperor
but one of the Ming Dynasty, who was now the
rightful heir to the throne. The rapidly growing
power of the Manchus had been lost sight of, if indeed
it had ever been thoroughly realised, and it seemed
quite natural that the representative of the House of
Ming should be put forward to resist the rebels.

This monarch, however, was quite unequal to the
fate which had befallen him ; and, before long, both
he himself and his capital were in the hands of the
Manchus. Other claimants to the throne appeared
in various places ; notably, one at Hangchow and
another at Foochow, each of whom looked upon the
other as a usurper. The former was soon disposed
of, but the latter gradually established his rule over
a wide area, and for a long time kept the Manchus
at bay, so hateful was the thought of an alien
domination to the people of the province in question.
Towards the close of 1646, he too had been captured,
and the work of pacification went on, the penalty
of death being now exacted in the case of officials
who refused to shave the head and wear the queue.
Two more Emperors, both of Imperial Ming blood,

were next proclaimed in Canton, one of whom strangled himself on the advance of the Manchus, while the other disappeared. A large number of loyal officials, rather than shave the front part of the head and wear the Manchu queue, voluntarily shaved the whole head, and sought sanctuary in monasteries, where they joined the Buddhist priesthood.

One more early attempt to re-establish the Mings must be noticed. The fourth son of a grandson of the Ming Emperor Wan Li (*died* 1620) was in 1646 proclaimed Emperor at Nan-yang in Honan. For a number of years of bloody warfare he managed to hold out ; but gradually he was forced to retire, first to Fuhkien and Kuangtung, and then into Kueichou and Yünnan, from which he was finally expelled by Wu San-kuei. He next fled to Burma, where in 1661 he was handed over to Wu San-kuei, who had followed in pursuit ; and he finally strangled himself in the capital of Yünnan. He is said to have been a Christian, as also many of his adherents ; in consequence of which, the Jesuit father, A. Koffler, bestowed upon him the title of the Constantine of China. In view of the general character for ferocity with which the Manchus are usually credited, it is pleasant to be able to record that when the official history of the Ming Dynasty came to be written, a Chinese scholar of the day, sitting on the historical commission, pleaded that three of the princes above mentioned, who were veritable scions of the Imperial stock, should be entered as " brave men " and not as " rebels," and that the Emperor, to whose reign we are now coming, graciously granted his request.

In the year 1661 Shun Chih, the first actual Emperor of the Ch'ing dynasty, " became a guest on high." He does not rank as one of China's great monarchs, but his kindly character as a man, and his magnanimity as a ruler, were extolled by his contemporaries. He treated the Catholic missionaries with favour. The Dutch and Russian embassies to his court in 1656 found there envoys from the Great Mogul, from the Western Tartars, and from the Dalai Lama. China, in the days when her civilization towered above that of most countries on the globe, and when her strength commanded the respect of all nations, great and small, was quite accustomed to receive embassies from foreign parts ; the first recorded instance being that of " An-tun " = Marcus Aurelius *Anton*inus, which reached China in A.D. 166. But because the tribute offered in this case contained no jewels, consisting merely of ivory, rhinoceros-horn, tortoise-shell, etc., which had been picked up in Annam, some have regarded it merely as a trading enterprise, and not really an embassy from the Roman Emperor ; Chinese writers, on

c

the other hand, suggest that the envoys sold the valuable jewels and bought a trumpery collection of tribute articles on the journey.

By the end of Shun Chih's reign, the Manchus, once a petty tribe of hardy bowmen, far beyond the outskirts of the empire, were in undoubted possession of all China, of Manchuria, of Korea, of most of Mongolia, and even of the island of Formosa. How this island, discovered by the Chinese only in 1430, became Manchu property, is a story not altogether without romance.

The leader of a large fleet of junks, traders or pirates as occasion served, known to the Portuguese of the day as Iquon, was compelled to place his services at the command of the last sovereign of the Ming dynasty, in whose cause he fought against the Manchu invaders along the coasts of Fuhkien and Kuangtung. In 1628 he tendered his submission to the Manchus, and for a time was well treated, and cleared the seas of other pirates. Gradually, however, he became too powerful, and it was deemed necessary to restrain him by force. He was finally induced to surrender to the Manchu general in Fuhkien; and having been made a prisoner, was sent to Peking, with two of his sons by a Japanese wife, together with other of his adherents, all of whom were executed upon arrival. Another son, familiar to foreigners under the name of Koxinga, a Portuguese corruption of his title, had remained behind with the fleet when his father surrendered, and he, determined to avenge his father's treacherous death, declared an implacable war against the Manchus. His piratical attacks on the coast of China had long been a terror to the inhabitants ; to such an extent, indeed, that the populations of no fewer than eighty townships had been forced to remove inland. Then Formosa, upon which the Dutch had begun to form colonies in 1634, and where substantial portions of their forts are still to be seen, attracted his piratical eye. He attacked the Dutch, and succeeded in driving them out with great slaughter, thus possessing himself of the island ; but gradually his followers began to drop off, in submission to the new dynasty, and at length he himself was reported to Peking as dead. In 1874, partly on the ground that he was really a supporter of the Ming dynasty and not a rebel, and partly on the ground that " he had founded in the midst of the waste of waters a dominion which he had transmitted to his descendants, and which was by them surrendered to the Imperial sway,"—a memorial was presented to the throne, asking that his spirit might be canonized as the guardian angel of Formosa, and that a shrine might be built in his honour. The request was granted.

Consolidation of the empire thus won by the

sword was carried out as follows.   In addition to the
large Manchu garrison at Peking, smaller garrisons
were established at nine of the provincial capitals,
and at ten other important points in the provinces.
The Manchu commandant of each of the nine
garrisons above mentioned, familiar to foreigners
as the Tartar General, was so placed in order to act
as a check upon the civil Governor or Viceroy,
of whom he, strictly speaking, took precedence,
though in practice their ranks have always been
regarded as equal.   With the empire at peace, the
post of Tartar General has always been a sinecure,
and altogether out of comparison with that of the
Viceroy and his responsibilities ; but in the case
of a Viceroy suspected of disloyalty and collusion
with rebels, the swift opportunity of the Tartar
General was the great safeguard of the dynasty,
further strengthened as he was by the regulation
which gave to him the custody of the keys to the
city gates.   Those garrisons, the soldiers of which
were accompanied by their wives and families, were
from the first intended to be permanent institutions ;
and there until quite recently were to be found the
descendants of the original drafts, not allowed to
intermarry with their Chinese neighbours, but
otherwise influenced to such an extent that their
Manchu characteristics had almost entirely disappeared.   In one direction the Manchus made a

curious concession which, though entirely sentimental, was nevertheless well calculated to appeal to a
proud though conquered people. A rule was established under which every Manchu high official, when
memorializing the throne, was to speak of himself to
the Emperor as "your Majesty's slave," whereas the
term accepted from every Chinese high official was
simply "your Majesty's servant." During the early
years of Manchu rule, proficiency in archery was as
much insisted on as in the days of Edward III with
us; and even down to a few years ago Manchu
Bannermen, as they came to be called, might be seen
everywhere diligently practising the art—actually
one of the six fine arts of China—by the aid of which
their ancestors had passed from the state of a petty
tribal community to possession of the greatest empire
in the world.

The term Bannerman, it may here be explained,
is applied to all Manchus in reference to their
organization under one or other of eight banners of
different colour and design; besides which, there
are also eight banners for Mongolians, and eight
more for the descendants of those Chinese who sided
with the Manchus against the Mings, and thus
helped to establish the Great Pure dynasty.

One of the first cares to the authorities of a newly-
established dynasty in China is to provide the
country with a properly authorized Penal Code, and

this has usually been accomplished by accepting as basis the code of the preceding rulers, and making such changes or modifications as may be demanded by the spirit of the times. It is generally understood that such was the method adopted under the first Manchu Emperor. The code of the Mings was carefully examined, its severities were softened, and various additions and alterations were made ; the result being a legal instrument which has received almost unqualified admiration from eminent Western lawyers. It has, however, been stated that the true source of the Manchu code must be looked for in the code of the T'ang dynasty (A.D. 618-905) ; possibly both codes were used. Within the compass of historical times, the country has never been without one, the first code having been drawn up by a distinguished statesman so far back as 525 B.C. In any case, at the beginning of the reign of Shun Chih a code was issued, which contained only certain fundamental and unalterable laws for the empire, with an Imperial preface, nominally from the hand of the Emperor himself. The next step was to supply any necessary additions and modifications ; and as time went on these were further amended or enlarged by Imperial decrees, founded upon current events,—a process which has been going on down to the present day. The code therefore consists of two parts : (1) immutable laws more or less embodying great principles beyond the reach of revision, and (2) a body of case-law which, since 1746, has been subject to revision every five years. With the publication of the Penal Code, the legal responsibilities of the new Emperor began and ended. There is not, and never has been, anything in China of the nature of civil law, beyond local custom and the application of common sense.

Towards the close of this reign, intercourse with China brought about an economic revolution in the West, especially in England, the importance of which it is difficult to realize sufficiently at this distant date. A new drink was put on the breakfast-table, destined to displace completely the quart of ale with which even Lady Jane Grey is said to have washed down her morning bacon. It is mentioned by Pepys, under the year 1660, as "tee (a China drink)," which he says he had never tasted before. Two centuries later, the export of tea from China had reached huge proportions, no less an amount than one hundred million *lb.* having been exported in one season from Foochow alone.

CHAPTER IV

K'ANG HSI

THE Emperor Shun Chih was succeeded by his third son, known by his year-title as K'ang Hsi (lasting prosperity), who was only eight years old at the time of his accession. Twelve years later the new monarch took up the reins of government, and soon began to make his influence felt. Fairly tall and well proportioned, he loved all manly exercises, and devoted three months annually to hunting. Large bright eyes lighted up his face, which was pitted with smallpox. Contemporary observers vie with one another in praising his wit, understanding, and liberality of mind. He was not twenty when the three feudatory princes broke into open rebellion. Of these, Wu San-kuei, the virtual founder of the dynasty, who had been appointed in 1659, was the chief; and it was at his instigation that his colleagues who ruled in Kuangtung and Fuhkien determined to throw off their allegiance and set up independent sovereignties. Within a few months, K'ang Hsi found vast portions of the empire slipping from his grasp; but though at one moment only the provinces of Chihli, Honan,

and Shantung were left to him in peaceable
possession, he never lost heart. The resources of
Wu San-kuei were ultimately found to be insufficient
for the struggle, the issue of which was determined
partly by his death in 1678, and partly by the
powerful artillery manufactured for the Imperial
forces by the Jesuit missionaries, who were then in
high favour at court. The capital city of Yünnan
was taken by assault in 1681, upon which Wu
San-kuei's son committed suicide, and the rebellion
collapsed. From that date the Manchus decided
that there should be no more " princes " among
their Chinese subjects, and the rule has been observed
until the present day.

Under the Emperor K'ang Hsi a re-arrangement
of the empire was planned and carried out ; that is
to say, whereas during the Mongol dynasty there
had only been thirteen provinces, increased to fifteen
by the Mings, there was now a further increase of
three, thus constituting what is known as the
Eighteen Provinces, or China Proper. To effect
this, the old province of Kiangnan was divided
into the modern Anhui and Kiangsu ; Kansuh was
carved out of Shensi ; and Hukuang was separated
into Hupeh and Hunan. Formosa, which was
finally reconquered in 1683, was made part of the
province of Fuhkien, and so remained for some two
hundred years, when it was erected into an inde-

pendent province. Thus, for a time China Proper consisted of nineteen provinces, until the more familiar " eighteen " was recently restored by the transfer of Formosa to Japan. In addition to the above, the eastern territory, originally inhabited by the Manchus, was divided into the three provinces already mentioned, all of which were at first organized upon a purely military basis ; but of late years the administration of the southernmost province, in which stands Mukden, the Manchu capital, has been brought more into line with that of China Proper.

In 1677 the East India Company established an agency at Amoy, which, though withdrawn in 1681, was re-established in 1685. The first treaty with Russia was negotiated in 1679, but less than ten years later a further treaty was found necessary, under which it was agreed that the river Amur was to be the boundary-line between the two dominions, the Russians giving up possession of both banks. Thus Ya-k'o-sa, or Albazin, was ceded by Russia to China, and some of the inhabitants, who appear to have been either pure Russians or half-castes, were sent as prisoners to Peking, where religious instruction was provided for them according to the rules of the orthodox church. All the descendants of these Albazins probably perished in the destruction of the Russian college during the siege of the Legations in 1900. Punitive expeditions against Galdan and Arabtan carried the frontiers of the empire to the borders of Khokand and Badakshan, and to the confines of Tibet.

Galdan was a khan of the Kalmucks, who succeeded in establishing his rule through nearly the whole of Turkestan, after attaining his position by the murder of a brother. He attacked the Khalkas, and thus incurred the resentment of K'ang Hsi, whose subjects they were ; and in order to strengthen his power, he applied to the Dalai Lama for ordination, but was refused. He then feigned conversion to Mahometanism, though without attracting Mahometan sympathies. In 1689 the Emperor in person led an army against him, crossing the deadly desert of Gobi for this purpose. Finally, after a further expedition and a decisive defeat in 1693, Galdan became a fugitive, and died three years afterwards. He was succeeded as khan by his nephew, Arabtan, who soon took up the offensive against China. He invaded Tibet, and pillaged the monasteries as far as Lhasa ; but was ultimately driven back by a Manchu army to Sungaria, where he was murdered in 1727.

The question of the calendar early attracted attention under the reign of K'ang Hsi. After the capture of Peking in 1644, the Manchus had employed the Jesuit Father, Schaal, upon the Astro-

nomical Board, an appointment which, owing to the
jealousies aroused, very nearly cost him his life.
What he taught was hardly superior to the astronomy
then in vogue, which had been inherited from the
Mongols, being nothing more than the old Ptolemaic
system, already discarded in Europe. In 1669, a
Flemish Jesuit Father from Courtrai, named Verbiest,
was placed upon the Board, and was entrusted
with the correction of the calendar according to more
recent investigations.

Christianity was officially recognized in 1692, and
an Imperial edict was issued ordering its toleration
throughout the empire. The discovery of the
Nestorian Tablet in 1625 had given a considerable
impulse, in spite of its heretical associations, to
Christian propagandism ; and it was estimated
that in 1627 there were no fewer than thirteen
thousand converts, many of whom were highly
placed officials, and even members of the Imperial
family. An important question, however, now came
to a head, and completely put an end to the hope
that China under the Manchus might embrace the
Roman Catholic faith. The question was this :
May converts to Christianity continue the worship
of ancestors ? Ricci, the famous Jesuit, who died
in 1610, and who is the only foreigner mentioned by
name in the dynastic histories of China, was inclined
to regard worship of ancestors more as a civil than a

religious rite. He probably foresaw, as indeed time
has shown, that ancestral worship would prove to be
an insuperable obstacle to many inquirers, if they
were called upon to discard it once and for all; at
the same time, he must have known that an invoca-
tion to spirits, coupled with the hope of obtaining
some benefit therefrom, is *worship* pure and simple,
and cannot be explained away as an unmeaning
ceremony.

Against the Jesuits in this matter were arrayed
the Dominicans and Franciscans; and the two
parties fought the question before several Popes,
sometimes one side carrying its point, and sometimes
the other. At length, in 1698, a fresh petition was
forwarded by the Jesuit order in China, asking the
Pope to sanction the practice of this rite by native
Christians, and also praying that the Chinese language
might be used in the celebration of mass. K'ang
Hsi supported the Jesuits in the view that ancestral
worship was a harmless ceremony; but after much
wrangling, and the dispatch of a Legate to the
Manchu court, the Pope decided against the Jesuits
and their Imperial ally. This was too much for the
pride of K'ang Hsi, and he forthwith declared that
in future he would only allow facilities for preaching
to those priests who shared his view. In 1716, an
edict was issued, banishing all missionaries unless
excepted as above. The Emperor had indeed been

annoyed by another ecclesiastical squabble, on a minor scale of importance, which had been raging almost simultaneously around the choice of an appropriate Chinese term for God. The term approved, if not suggested, by K'ang Hsi, and indisputably the right one, as shown by recent research, was set aside by the Pope in 1704 in favour of one which was supposed for a long time to have been coined for the purpose, but which had really been applied for many centuries previously to one of the eight spirits of ancient mythology.

In addition to his military campaign, K'ang Hsi carried out several journeys of considerable length, and managed to see something of the empire beyond the walls of Peking. He climbed the famous mountain, T'ai-shan, in Shantung, the summit of which had been reached in 219 B.C. by the famous First Emperor, burner of the books and part builder of the Great Wall, and where a century later another Emperor had instituted a mysterious worship of Heaven and Earth. The ascent of T'ai-shan had been previously accomplished by only six Emperors in all, the last of whom went up in the year 1008 ; since K'ang Hsi no further Imperial attempts have been made, so that his will close the list in connexion with the Manchu dynasty. It was on this occasion too that he visited the tomb of Confucius, also in Shantung.

The vagaries of the Yellow River, named " China's Sorrow " by a later Emperor, were always a source of great anxiety to K'ang Hsi ; so much so that he paid a personal visit to the scene, and went carefully into the various plans for keeping the waters to a given course. Besides causing frequently recurring floods, with immense loss of life and property, this river has a way of changing unexpectedly its bed ; so lately as 1856, it turned off at right angles near the city of K'ai-fêng, in Honan, and instead of emptying itself into the Yellow Sea about latitude 34°, found a new outlet in the Gulf of Peichili, latitude 38°.

K'ang Hsi several times visited Hangchow, re-turning to Tientsin by the Grand Canal, a distance of six hundred and ninety miles. This canal, it will be remembered, was designed and executed under Kublai Khan in the thirteenth century, and helped to form an almost unbroken line of water communication between Peking and Canton. At Hangchow, during one visit, he held an examination of all the (so-called) B.A.'s and M.A.'s, especially to test their poetical skill ; and he also did the same at Soochow and Nanking, taking the opportunity, while at Nanking, to visit the mausoleum of the founder of the Ming dynasty, who lies buried near by, and whose descendants had been displaced by the

Manchus. Happily for K'ang Hsi's complacency, the book of fate is hidden from Emperors, as well as from subjects,—

All but the page prescribed, their present state

and he was unable to foresee another visit paid to that mausoleum two hundred and seven years later, under very different conditions, to which we shall come in due course.

The census has always been an important institution in China. Without going back so far as the legendary golden age, the statistics of which have been invented by enthusiasts, we may accept unhesitatingly such records as we find subsequent to the Christian era, on the understanding that these returns are merely approximate. They could hardly be otherwise, inasmuch as the Chinese count families and not heads, roughly allowing five souls to each household. This plan yields a total of rather over fifty millions for the year A.D. 156, and one hundred and five millions for the fortieth year of the reign of K'ang Hsi, 1701.

No record of this Emperor, however brief, could fail to notice the literary side of his character, and his extraordinary achievements in this direction. It is almost paradoxical, though absolutely true, that two Manchu Emperors, sprung from a race which but a few decades before had little thought for anything beyond war and the chase, and which had not even a written language of its own, should have conferred more benefits upon the student of literature than all the rest of China's Emperors put together. The literature in question is, of course, Chinese literature. Manchu was the court language, spoken as well as written, for many years after 1644, and down to quite recent times all official documents were in duplicate, one copy in Chinese and one in Manchu ; but a Manchu literature can hardly be said to exist, beyond translations of all the most important Chinese works. The Manchu dynasty is an admirable illustration of the old story : conquerors taken captive by the conquered.

At this moment, the term " K'ang Hsi " is daily on the lips of every student of the Chinese language, native or foreign, throughout the empire. This is due to the fact that the Emperor caused to be produced under his own personal superintendence, on a more extensive scale and a more systematic plan than any previous work of the kind, a lexicon of the Chinese language, containing over forty thousand characters, with numerous illustrative phrases chronologically arranged, the spelling of each character according to the method introduced by Buddhist teachers and first used in the third century, the tones, various readings, etc., etc., altogether a great work and still without a rival at the present day.

D

It would be tedious even to enumerate all the
various literary undertakings conceived and carried
out under the direction of K'ang Hsi ; but there
are two works in particular which cannot be passed
over. One of these is the huge illustrated encyclo-
pædia in which everything which has ever been said
upon each of a vast array of subjects is brought into
a systematized book of reference, running to many
hundred volumes, and being almost a complete
library in itself. It was printed, after the death of
K'ang Hsi, from movable copper types. The other
is, if anything, a still more extraordinary though not
such a voluminous work. It is a concordance to all
literature ; not of words, but of phrases. A student
meeting with an unfamiliar combination of characters can turn to its pages and find every passage
given, in sufficient fullness, where the phrase in
question has been used by poet, historian, or
essayist.

The last years of K'ang Hsi were beclouded by
family troubles. For some kind of intrigue, in which
magic played a prominent part, he had been compelled to degrade the Heir Apparent, and to appoint
another son to the vacant post ; but a year or two
later, this son was found to be mentally deranged,
and was placed under restraint. So things went on
for several more years, the Emperor apparently
unable to make up his mind as to the choice of a

successor ; and it was not until the last day of his life that he finally decided in favour of his fourth son. Dying in 1723, his reign had already extended beyond the Chinese cycle of sixty years, a feat which no Emperor of China, in historical times, had ever before achieved, but which was again to be accomplished, before the century was out, by his grandson.

CHAPTER V

THE fourth son of Kʻang Hsi came to the throne under the year-title of Yung Chêng (harmonious rectitude). He was confronted with serious difficulties from the very first. Dissatisfaction prevailed among his numerous brothers, at least one of whom may have felt that he had a better claim to rule than his junior in the family. This feeling culminated in a plot to dethrone Yung Chêng, which was, however, discovered in time, and resulted only in the degradation of the guilty brothers. The fact that among his opponents were native Christians—some say that the Jesuits were at the bottom of all the mischief—naturally influenced the Emperor against Christianity; no fewer than three hundred churches were destroyed, and all Catholic missionaries were thenceforward obliged to live either at Peking or at Macao. In 1732 he thought of expelling them altogether; but finding that they were enthusiastic teachers of filial piety, he left them alone, merely prohibiting fresh recruits from coming to China.

These domestic troubles were followed by a serious

rebellion in Kokonor, which was not fully suppressed until the next reign ; also by an outbreak among the aborigines of Kueichow and Yünnan, which lasted until three years later, when the tribesmen were brought under Imperial rule.

A Portuguese envoy, named Magalhaens (or Magaillans), visited Peking in 1727, bearing presents for the Emperor ; but nothing very much resulted from his mission. In 1730, in addition to terrible floods, there was a severe earthquake, which lasted ten days, and in which one hundred thousand persons are said to have lost their lives. In 1735, Yung Chêng's reign came to an end amid sounds of a further outbreak of the aborigines in Kueichow. Before his death, he named his fourth son, then only fifteen, as his successor, under the regency of two of the boy's uncles and two Grand Secretaries, one of the latter being a distinguished scholar, who was entrusted with the preparation of the history of the Ming dynasty. Yung Chêng's name has always been somewhat unfairly associated by foreigners with a bitter hostility to the Catholic priests of his day, simply because he refused to allow them a free hand in matters outside their proper sphere. Altogether, it may be said that he was a just and public-spirited ruler, anxious for his people's welfare. He hated war, and failed to carry on his father's vigorous policy in Central Asia ; nevertheless, by 1730,

Chinese rule extended to the Laos border, and the Shan States paid tribute. He was a man of letters, and completed some of his father's undertakings.

Yung Chêng's successor was twenty-five years of age when he came to the throne with the year-title of Ch'ien Lung (or Kien Long=enduring glory), and one of his earliest acts was to forbid the propagation of Christian. doctrine, a prohibition which developed between 1746 and 1785 into active persecution of its adherents. The first ten years of this reign were spent chiefly in internal reorganization; the remainder, which covered half a century, was almost a continuous succession of wars. The aborigines of Kueichow, known as the Miao-tzŭ, offered a determined resistance to all attempts to bring them under the regular administration; and although they were ultimately conquered, it was deemed advisable not to insist upon the adoption of the queue, and also to leave them a considerable measure of self-government. Acting under Manchu guidance, chiefs and leading tribesmen were entrusted with important executive offices; they had to keep the peace among their people, and to collect the revenue of local produce to be forwarded to Peking. These posts were hereditary. On the death of the father, the eldest son proceeded to Peking and received his appointment in person, together with his seal of office. Failing sons or their children, brothers had the right of succession.

In 1741 the population was estimated by Père Amiot, S.J., at over one hundred and fifty millions, as against twenty-one million households in 1701.

In 1753 there was trouble in Ili. After the death of Galdan II., son of Arabtan, an attempt was made by one, Amursana, to usurp the principality. He was, however, driven out, and fled to Peking, where he was favourably received by Ch'ien Lung, and an army was sent to reinstate him. With the subsequent settlement, under which he was to have only one quarter of Ili, Amursana was profoundly dissatisfied, and took the earliest opportunity of turning on his benefactors. He murdered the Manchu-Chinese garrison and all the other Chinese he could find, and proclkimed himself khan of the Eleuths. His triumph was short-lived ; another army was sent from Peking, this time against him, and he fled into Russian territory, dying there soon afterwards of smallpox. This campaign was lavishly illustrated by Chinese artists, who produced a series of realistic pictures of the battles and skirmishes fought by Ch'ien Lung's victorious troops. How far these were prepared under the guidance of the Jesuit Fathers does not seem to be known. About sixty years previously, under the reign of K'ang Hsi, the Jesuits had carried out extensive surveys, and had drawn fairly accurate maps of Chinese territory, which had been sent to Paris and there engraved on copper by order of Louis XIV. In like manner, the pictures now in question were forwarded to Paris and engraved, between 1769 and 1774, by skilled draughtsmen, as may be gathered from the lettering at the foot of each ; for instance—*Gravé par J. P. Le Bas, graveur du cabinet du roi* (Cambridge University Library).

Kuldja and Kashgaria were next added to the empire, and Manchu supremacy was established in Tibet. Burma and Nepal were forced to pay tribute, after a disastrous war (1766-1770) with the former country, in which a Chinese army had been almost exterminated ; rebellions in Ssŭch'uan (1770), Shantung (1777), and Formosa (1786) were suppressed.

Early in the eighteenth century, the Turguts, a branch of the Kalmuck Tartars, unable to endure the oppressive tyranny of their rulers, trekked into Russia, and settled on the banks of the Volga. Some seventy years later, once more finding the burden of taxation too heavy, they again organized a trek upon a colossal scale. Turning their faces eastward, they spent a whole year of fearful suffering and privation in reaching the confines of Ili, a terribly diminished host. There they received a district, and were placed under the jurisdiction of a khan. This journey has been dramatically described by De Quincey in an essay entitled " Revolt of the Tartars, or Flight of the Kalmuck Khan and his people from the Russian territories to the Frontiers of China." Of this contribution to literature it is only necessary to remark that the scenes described, and especially the numbers mentioned, must be credited chiefly to the perfervid imagination of the essayist, and also to certain not very trustworthy documents sent home by Père Amiot. It is probable that about one hundred and sixty thousand Turguts set out on that long march, of whom only some seventy thousand reached their goal.

In 1781, the Dungans (or Tungans) of Shensi broke into open rebellion, which was suppressed only after huge losses to the Imperialists. These Dungans were Mahometan subjects of China, who in very early times had colonized, under the name of Gao-tchan, in Kansuh and Shensi, and subsequently spread westward into Turkestan. Some say that they were a distinct race, who, in the fifth and sixth centuries, occupied the Tian Shan range, with their capital at Harashar. The name, however, means, in the dialect of Chinese Tartary, " converts," that is, to Mahometanism, to which they were converted in the days of Timour by an Arabian adventurer. We shall hear of them again in a still more serious connexion.

Eight years later there was a revolution in Cochin-China. The king fled to China, and Ch'ien Lung promptly espoused his cause, sending an army to effect his restoration. This was no sooner accomplished than the chief Minister rebelled, and, rapidly attracting large numbers to his standard, succeeded in cutting off the retreat of the Chinese force. Ch'ien Lung then sent another army, whereupon the rebel Minister submitted, and humbled himself so completely that the Emperor appointed him to be king instead of the other. After this, the Annamese continued to forward tribute, but it was deemed advisable to cease from further interference with their government.

The next trouble was initiated by the Gurkhas, who, in 1790, raided Tibet. On being defeated and pursued by a Chinese army, they gave up all the booty taken, and entered into an agreement to pay tribute once every five years.

The year 1793 was remarkable for the arrival of an English embassy under Lord Macartney, who was received in audience by the Emperor at Jehol (=hot river), an Imperial summer residence lying about a hundred miles north of Peking, beyond the Great Wall. It had been built in 1780 after the model of the palace of the Panshen Erdeni at Tashilumbo, in

Tibet, when that functionary, the spiritual ruler of
Tibet, as opposed to the Dalai Lama, who is the
secular ruler, proceeded to Peking to be present on
the seventieth anniversary of Ch'ien Lung's birth-
day. Two years later, the aged Emperor, who had,
like his grandfather, completed his cycle of sixty
years on the throne, abdicated in favour of his son,
dying in retirement four years after. These two
monarchs, K'ang Hsi and Ch'ien Lung, were among
the ablest, not only of Manchu rulers, but of any
whose lot it has been to shape the destinies of China.
Ch'ien Lung was an indefatigable administrator, a
little too ready perhaps to plunge into costly
military expeditions, and somewhat narrow in the
policy he adopted towards the " outside barbarians "
who came to trade at Canton and elsewhere, but
otherwise a worthy rival of his grandfather's fame
as a sovereign and patron of letters. From the
long list of works, mostly on a very extensive scale,
produced under his supervision, may be mentioned
the new and revised editions of the Thirteen Classics
of Confucianism and of the Twenty-four Dynastic
Histories. In 1772 a search was instituted under
Imperial orders for all literary works worthy of pre-
servation, and high provincial officials vied with
one another in forwarding rare and important works
to Peking. The result was the great descriptive
Catalogue of the Imperial Library, arranged under

the four heads of Classics (Confucianism), History,
Philosophy, and General Literature, in which all
the facts known about each work are set forth,
coupled with judicious critical remarks,—an achievement which has hardly a parallel in any literature
in the world.

CHAPTER VI

CHIA CH'ING

CH'IEN LUNG'S son, who reigned as Chia Ch'ing (high felicity—not to be confounded with Chia Ching of the Ming dynasty, 1522-1567), found himself in difficulties from the very start. The year of his accession was marked by a rising of the White Lily Society, one of the dreaded secret associations with which China is, and always has been, honeycombed. The exact origin of this particular society is not known. A White Lily Society was formed in the second century A.D. by a certain Taoist patriarch, and eighteen members were accustomed to assemble at a temple in modern Kiangsi for purposes of meditation. But this seems to have no connexion with the later sect, of which we first hear in 1308, when its existence was prohibited, its shrines destroyed, and its votaries forced to return to ordinary life. Members of the fraternity were then believed to possess a knowledge of the black art ; and later on, in 1622, the society was confounded by Chinese officials in Shantung with Christianity. In the present instance, it is said that no fewer than thirty thousand adherents were executed before the trouble was finally suppressed ; from which statement it is easy to gather that under whatever form the White Lily Society may have been originally initiated, its activities were now of a much more serious character, and were, in fact, plainly directed against the power and authority of the Manchus.

Almost from this very date may be said to have begun that turn of the tide which was to reach its flood a hundred years afterwards. The Manchus came into power, as conquerors by force of arms, at a time when the mandate of the previous dynasty had been frittered away in corruption and misrule ; and although to the Chinese eye they were nothing more than " stinking Tartars," there were not wanting many glad enough to see a change of rule at any price. Under the first Emperor, Shun Chih, there was barely time to find out what the new dynasty was going to do ; then came the long and glorious reign of K'ang Hsi, followed, after the thirteen harmless years of Yung Chêng, by the equally long and equally glorious reign of Ch'ien Lung. The Chinese people, who, strictly speaking, govern themselves in the most democratic of all republics, have not the slightest objection to the Imperial tradition, which has indeed been their continuous heritage from remotest antiquity, provided that public liberties are duly safeguarded, chiefly in the sense that there shall always be equal opportunities for all. They are quick to discover the character of their rulers, and discovery in an unfavourable direction leads to an early alteration of popular thought and demeanour. At the beginning of the seventeenth century, they had tired of eunuch oppression and unjust taxation, and they naturally hailed the genuine attempt in 1662 to get rid of eunuchs altogether, coupled with the persistent efforts of K'ang Hsi, and later of Ch'ien Lung, to lighten the burdens of revenue which weighed down the energies of all. But towards the end of his reign Ch'ien Lung had become a very old man ; and the gradual decay of his powers of personal supervision opened a way for the old abuses to creep in, bringing in their train the usual accompaniment of popular discontent.

The Emperor Chia Ch'ing, a worthless and dissolute ruler, never commanded the confidence of his people as his great predecessors had done, nor had he the same confidence in them. This want of mutual trust was not confined to his Chinese subjects only. In 1799, Ho-shên, a high Manchu official who had been raised by Ch'ien Lung from an obscure position to be a Minister of State and Grand Secretary, was suspected, probably without a shadow of evidence, of harbouring designs upon the throne. He was seized and tried, nominally for corruption and undue familiarity, and was condemned to death, being allowed as an act of grace to commit suicide.

In 1803 the Emperor was attacked in the streets of Peking ; and ten years later there was a serious outbreak organized by a secret society in Honan, known as the Society of Divine Justice, and alternatively as the White Feather Society, from the badge worn by those members who took part in the actual movement, which happened as follows. An attack upon the palace during the Emperor's absence on a visit to the Imperial tombs was arranged by the leaders, who represented a considerable body of malcontents, roused by the wrongs which their countrymen were suffering all over the empire at the hands of their Manchu rulers. By promises of large rewards and appointments to lucrative offices when the Manchus should be got rid of, the collusion of a number of the eunuchs was secured ; and on a given day some four hundred rebels, disguised as villagers carrying baskets of fruit in which arms were concealed, collected about the gates of the palace. Some say that one of the leaders was betrayed, others that the eunuchs made a mistake in the date ; at any rate there was a sudden rush on the part of the conspirators, the guards at the gates were overpowered, every one who was not wearing a white feather was cut down, and the palace seemed to be at the mercy of the rebels. The latter, however, were met by a desperate resistance from the young princes, who shot down several of them, and thus alarmed the soldiers. Assistance was promptly at hand, and the rebels were all killed or captured. Immediate measures were taken to suppress the Society, of which it is said that over twenty thousand members were executed, and as many more sent in exile to Ili.

Not one, however, of the numerous secret societies, which from time to time have flourished in China, can compare for a moment either in numbers or organization with the formidable association known as the Heaven and Earth Society, and also as the Triad Society, or Hung League, which dates from the reign of Yung Chêng, and from first to last has had one definite aim,—the overthrow of the Manchu dynasty.

The term " Triad " signifies the harmonious union of heaven (q.d. God), earth, and man ; and members of the fraternity communicate to one another the fact of membership by pointing first up to the sky, then down to the ground, and last to their own hearts. The Society was called the Hung League, because all the members adopted Hung as a surname, a word which suggests the idea of a cataclysm. By a series of lucky chances the inner working of this Society became known about fifty years ago, when a

E

mass of manuscripts containing the history of the
Society, its ritual, oaths, and secret signs, together
with an elaborate set of drawings of flags and other
regalia, fell into the hands of the Dutch Government
at Batavia.   These documents, translated by Dr G.
Schlegel, disclose an extraordinary similarity in
many respects between the working of Chinese lodges
and the working of those which are more familiar
to us as temples of the Ancient Order of Free and
Accepted Masons.   Such points of contact, however,
as may be discoverable, are most probably mere
coincidences ; if not, and if, as is generally understood, the ritual of the European craft was concocted by Cagliostro, then it follows that he must
have borrowed from the Chinese, and not the
Chinese from him.   The use of the square and com-
passes as symbols of moral rectitude, which forms
such a striking feature of European masonry, finds
no place in the ceremonial of the Triad Society,
although recognized as such in Chinese literature
from the days of Confucius, and still so employed
in the every-day colloquial of China.

In 1816 Lord Amherst's embassy reached Peking.
Its object was to secure some sort of arrangement
under which British merchants might carry on trade
after a more satisfactory manner than had been
the case hitherto.   The old Co-hong, a system first
established in 1720, under which certain Chinese

merchants at Canton became responsible to the local authorities for the behaviour of the English merchants, and to the latter for all debts due to them, had been so complicated by various oppressive laws, that at one time the East India Company had threatened to stop all business. Lord Amherst, however, accomplished nothing in the direction of reform. From the date of his landing at Tientsin, he was persistently told that unless he agreed to perform the *kotow*, he could not possibly be admitted to an audience. It was probably his equally persistent refusal to do so—a ceremonial which had been excused by Ch'ien Lung in the case of Lord Macartney—that caused the Ministers to change their tactics, and to declare, on Lord Amherst's arrival at the Summer Palace, tired and wayworn, that the Emperor wished to see him immediately. Not only had the presents, of which he was the bearer, not arrived at the palace, but he and his suite, among whom were Sir George Stanton, Dr Morrison, and Sir John Davis, had not received the trunks containing their uniforms. It was therefore impossible for the ambassador to present himself before the Emperor, and he flatly refused to do so ; whereupon he received orders to proceed at once to the sea-coast, and take himself off to his own country. A curious comment on this fiasco was made by Napoleon, who thought that the English

Government had acted wrongly in not having ordered Lord Amherst to comply with the custom of the place he was sent to ; otherwise, he should not have been sent at all. " It is my opinion that whatever is the custom of a nation, and is practised by the first characters of that nation towards their chief, cannot degrade strangers who perform the same."

In 1820 Chia Ch'ing died, after a reign of twenty-five years, notable, if for nothing else, as marking the beginning of Manchu decadence, evidence of which is to be found in the unusually restless temper of the people, and even in such apparent trifles as the abandonment of the annual hunting excursions, always before carried out on an extensive scale, and presenting, as it were, a surviving indication of former Manchu hardihood and personal courage. He was succeeded by his second son, who was already forty years of age, and whose hitherto secluded life had ill-prepared him for the difficult problems he was shortly called upon to face.

CHAPTER VII

TAO KUANG

TAO KUANG (glory of right principle), as he is called, from the style chosen for his reign, gave promise of being a useful and enlightened ruler ; at the least a great improvement on his father. He did his best at first to purify the court, but his natural indolence stood in the way of any real reform, and with the best intentions in the world he managed to leave the empire in a still more critical condition than that in which he had found it. Five years after his accession, his troubles began in real earnest. There was a rising of the people in Kashgaria, due to criminal injustice practised over a long spell of time on the part of the Chinese authorities. The rebels found a leader in the person of Jehangir, who claimed descent from one of the old native chiefs, formerly recognized by the Manchu Emperors, but now abolished as such. Thousands flocked to his standard ; and by the time an avenging army could arrive on the scene, he was already master of the country. During the campaign which followed, his men were defeated in battle after battle ; and at length he himself was taken prisoner and forwarded to Peking, where he failed to defend his conduct, and was put to death.

The next serious difficulty which confronted the Emperor was a rising, in 1832, of the wild Miao tribes of Kuangsi and Hunan, led by a man who either received or adopted the title of the Golden Dragon. At the bottom of all the trouble we find, as usually to be expected henceforward, the secret activities of the far-reaching Triad Society, which seized the occasion to foment into open rebellion the dissatisfaction of the tribesmen with the glaring injustice they were suffering at the hands of the local authorities. After some initial massacres and reprisals, a general was sent to put an end to the outbreak ; but so far from doing this, he seems to have come off second best in most of the battles which ensued, and was finally driven into Kuangtung. For this he was superseded, and two Commissioners dispatched to take charge of further operations. It occurred to these officials that possibly persuasion might succeed where violence had failed; and accordingly a proclamation was widely circulated, promising pardon and redress of wrongs to all who would at once return to their allegiance, and pointing out at the same time the futility of further resistance. The effect of this move was magical ; within a few days the rebellion was over.

We are now reaching a period at which European complications began to be added to the more legitimate worries of a Manchu Emperor. Trade with the Portuguese, the Spaniards, the Dutch, and the English, had been carried on since the early years of the sixteenth century, but in a very haphazard kind of way, and under many vexatious restrictions, bribery being the only effectual means of bringing commercial ventures to a successful issue. So far back as 1680, the East India Company had received its charter, and commercial relations with Chinese merchants could be entered into by British subjects only through this channel. Such machinery answered its purpose very well for a long period ; but a monopoly of the kind became out of date as time went on, and in 1834 it ceased altogether. The Company was there for the sake of trade, and for nothing else ; and one of its guiding principles was avoidance of any acts which might wound Chinese susceptibilities, and tend to defeat the object of its own existence. Consequently, the directors would not allow opium to be imported in their vessels ; neither were they inclined to patronize missionary efforts. It is true that Morrison's dictionary was printed at the expense of the Company, when the punishment for a native teaching a foreigner the Chinese language was death ; but no pecuniary assistance was forthcoming when the same distinguished missionary attempted to translate the Bible for distribution in China.

The Manchus, who had themselves entered the country as robbers of the soil and spoliators of the people, were determined to do their best to keep out all future intruders ; and it was for this reason that, suspicious of the aims of the barbarian, every possible obstacle was placed in the way of those who wished to learn to speak and read Chinese. This suspicion was very much increased in the case of missionaries, whose real object the Manchus failed to appreciate, and behind whose plea of religious propagandism they thought they detected a deep-laid scheme for territorial aggression, to culminate of course in their own overthrow ; and already in 1805 an edict had been issued, strictly forbidding anyone to teach even Manchu to any foreigner.

From this date (1834), any British subject was free to engage in the trade, and the Home Government sent out Lord Napier to act as Chief Superintendent, and to enter into regular diplomatic relations with the Chinese authorities. Lord Napier, however, even though backed by a couple of frigates, was unable to gain admission to the city of Canton, and after a demonstration, the only result of which was to bring all business to a standstill, he was

finally obliged in the general interest to retire. He
went to Macao, a small peninsula to the extreme
south-west of the Kuangtung province, famous as
the residence of the poet Camoens, and there he died
a month later. Macao was first occupied by the
Portuguese trading with China in 1557; though
there is a story that in 1517 certain Portuguese
landed there under pretence of drying some tribute
presents to the Emperor, which had been damaged
in a storm, and proceeded to fortify their encamp-
ment, whereupon the local officials built a wall across
the peninsula, shutting off further access to the main-
land. It also appears that, in 1566, Macao was
actually ceded to the Portuguese on condition of
payment of an annual sum to China, which payment
ceased after trouble between the two countries in
1849.

The next few years were employed by the successors
of Lord Napier in endeavours, often wrongly directed,
to establish working, if not harmonious, relations
with the Chinese authorities; but no satisfactory
point was reached, for the simple reason that recent
events had completely confirmed the officials and
people in their old views as to the relative status
of the barbarians and themselves.

It is worth noticing here that Russia, with her
conterminous and ever-advancing frontier, has always
been regarded somewhat differently from the oversea

barbarian. She has continually during the past
three centuries been the dreaded foreign bogy of
the Manchus ; and a few years back, when Manchus
and Chinese alike fancied that their country was
going to be " chopped up like a melon " and divided
among western nations, a warning geographical
cartoon was widely circulated in China, showing
Russia in the shape of a huge bear stretching down
from the north and clawing the vast areas of Mongolia
and Manchuria to herself.

Now, to aggravate the already difficult situation,
the opium question came suddenly to the front in an
acute form. For a long time the import of opium
had been strictly forbidden by the Government, and
for an equally long time smuggling the drug in
increasing quantities had been carried on in a most
determined manner until, finally, swift vessels with
armed crews, sailing under foreign flags, succeeded
in terrorizing the native revenue cruisers, and so
delivering their cargoes as they pleased. It appears
that the Emperor Tao Kuang, who had sounded the
various high authorities on the subject, was genuinely
desirous of putting an end to the import of opium,
and so checking the practice of opium-smoking,
which was already assuming dangerous proportions ;
and in this he was backed up by Captain Elliot
(afterwards Sir Charles Elliot), now Superintendent
of Trade, an official whose vacillating policy towards

the Chinese authorities did much to precipitate the disasters about to follow. After a serious riot had been provoked, in which the foreign merchants of Canton narrowly escaped with their lives, and to quell which it was necessary to call out the soldiery, the Emperor decided to put a definite stop to the opium traffic ; and for this purpose he appointed one of his most distinguished servants, at that time Viceroy of Hukuang, and afterwards generally known as Commissioner Lin, a name much reverenced by the Chinese as that of a true patriot, and never mentioned even by foreigners without respect. Early in 1839, Lin took up the post of Viceroy of Kuangtung, and immediately initiated an attack which, to say the least of it, deserved a better fate.

Within a few days a peremptory order was made for the delivery of all opium in the possession of foreign merchants at Canton. This demand was resisted, but for a short time only. All the foreign merchants, together with Captain Elliot, who had gone up to Canton specially to meet the crisis, found themselves prisoners in their own houses, deprived of servants and even of food. Then Captain Elliot undertook, on behalf of his Government, to indemnify British subjects for their losses ; whereupon no fewer than twenty thousand two hundred and ninety-one chests of opium were surrendered to Commissioner

Lin, and the incident was regarded by the Chinese as closed. On receipt of the Emperor's instructions, the whole of this opium, for which the owners received orders on the Treasury at the rate of £120 per chest, was mixed with lime and salt water, and was entirely destroyed.

Lin's subsequent demands were so arbitrary that at length the English mercantile community retired altogether from Canton, and after a futile attempt to settle at Macao, where their presence, owing to Chinese influence with the Portuguese occupiers, was made unwelcome, they finally found a refuge at Hongkong, then occupied only by a few fishermen's huts. Further negotiations as to the renewal of trade having fallen through, Lin gave orders for all British ships to leave China within three days, which resulted in a fight between two men-of-war and twenty-nine war-junks, in which the latter were either sunk or driven off with great loss. In June, 1840, a British fleet of seventeen men-of-war and twenty-seven troopships arrived at Hongkong; Canton was blockaded; a port on the island of Chusan was subsequently occupied; and Lord Palmerston's letter to the Emperor was carried to Tientsin, and delivered there to the Viceroy of Chihli. Commissioner Lin was now cashiered for incompetency; but was afterwards instructed to act with the Viceroy of Chihli, who was sent down to

supersede him. Further vexatious action, or rather
inaction, on the part of these two at length drove
Captain Elliot to an ultimatum ; and as no attention
was paid to this; the Bogue forts near the mouth of
the Canton river were taken by the British fleet,
after great slaughter of the Chinese. In January,
1841, a treaty of peace was arranged, under which
the island of Hongkong was to be ceded to England,
a sum of over a million pounds was to be paid for the
opium destroyed, and satisfactory concessions were
to be made in the matter of official intercourse between
the two nations. The Emperor refused ratification,
and ordered the extermination of the barbarians
to be at once proceeded with. Again the Bogue
forts were captured, and Canton would have been
occupied but for another promised treaty, the terms
of which were accepted by Sir Henry Pottinger, who
now superseded Elliot. At this juncture the British
fleet sailed northwards, capturing Amoy and Ningpo,
and occupying the island of Chusan. The further
capture of Chapu, where munitions of war in huge
quantities were destroyed, was followed by similar
successes at Shanghai and Chinkiang. At the last-
mentioned, a desperate resistance was offered by
the Manchu garrison, who fought heroically against
certain defeat, and who, when all hope was gone,
committed suicide in large numbers rather than fall
into the hands of the enemy, from whom, in accord-

ance with prevailing ideas and with what would
have been their own practice, they expected no
quarter. The Chinese troops, as distinguished from
the Manchus, behaved differently ; they took to
their heels before a shot had been fired. This
behaviour, which seems to be nothing more than
arrant cowardice, is nevertheless open to a more
favourable interpretation. The yoke of the Manchu
dynasty was already beginning to press heavily, and
these men felt that they had no particular cause
to fight for, certainly not such a personal cause as
then stared the Manchus in the face. The Manchu
soldiers were fighting for their all : their very
supremacy was at stake ; while many of the Chinese
troops were members of the Triad Society, the
chief object of which was to get rid of the alien
dynasty. It is thus, too, that we can readily
explain the assistance afforded to the enemy by
numerous Cantonese, and the presence of many
as servants on board the vessels of our fleet ;
they did not help us or accompany us from any
lack of patriotism, of which virtue Chinese annals
have many striking examples to show, but because
they were entirely out of sympathy with their
rulers, and would have been glad to see them
overthrown, coupled of course with the tempt-
ing pay and good treatment offered by the
barbarian.

It now remained to take Nanking, and thither the fleet proceeded in August, 1842, with that purpose in view. This move the Chinese authorities promptly anticipated by offering to come to terms in a friendly way ; and in a short time conditions of peace were arranged under an important instrument, known as the Treaty of Nanking. Its chief clauses provided for the opening to British trade of Canton, Amoy, Foochow, Ningpo, and Shanghai, at which all British subjects were to enjoy the rights of extra-territoriality, being subject to the jurisdiction of their own officials only; also, for the cession to England of the island of Hongkong, and for the pay-ment of a lump sum of about five million pounds as compensation for loss of opium, expenses of the war, etc. All prisoners were to be released, and there was a special amnesty for such Chinese as had given their services to the British during the war. An equality of status between the officials of both nations was further conceded, and suitable rules were to be drawn up for the regulation of trade. The above treaty having been duly ratified by Tao Kuang and by Queen Victoria, it must then have seemed to British merchants that a new and prosperous era had really dawned. But they counted without the ever-present desire of the great bulk of the Chinese people to see the last of the Manchus ; and the Triad Society, stimulated no doubt by the recent British successes, had already shown signs of unusual activity when, in 1850, the Emperor died, and was succeeded by his fourth son, who reigned under the title of Hsien Fêng (or Hien Fong=universal plenty).

CHAPTER VIII

HSIEN FÊNG

HSIEN FÊNG came to the throne at the age of nineteen, and found himself in possession of a heritage which showed evident signs of going rapidly to pieces. His father, in the opinion of many competent Chinese, had been sincerely anxious for the welfare of his country ; on the other hand, he had failed to learn anything from the lessons he had received at the hands of foreigners, towards whom his attitude to the last was of the bow-wow order. On one occasion, indeed, he borrowed a classical phrase, and referring to the intrusions of the barbarians, declared roundly that he would allow no man to snore alongside of his bed. Brought up in this spirit, Hsien Fêng had already begun to exhibit an anti-foreign bias, when he found himself in the throes of a struggle which speedily reduced the European question to quite insignificant proportions.

A clever young Cantonese, named Hung Hsiu-ch'üan, from whom great things were expected, failed, in 1833, to secure the first degree at the usual public examination. Four years later, when twenty-four years of age, he made another attempt, only,

F

however, to be once more rejected. Chagrin at this second failure brought on melancholia, and he began to see visions ; and later on, while still in this depressed state of mind, he turned his attention to some Christian tracts which had been given to him on his first appearance at the examination, but which he had so far allowed to remain unread. In these he discovered what he thought were interpretations of his earlier dreams, and soon managed to persuade himself that he had been divinely chosen to bring to his countrymen a knowledge of the true God.

In one sense this would only have been reversion to a former condition, for in ancient times a simple monotheism formed the whole creed of the Chinese people ; but Hung went much further, and after having become head of a Society of God, he started a sect of professing Christians, and set to work to collect followers, styling himself the Brother of Christ. Gradually, the authorities became aware of his existence, and also of the fact that he was drawing together a following on a scale which might prove dangerous to the public peace. It was then that force of circumstances changed his status from that of a religious reformer to that of a political adventurer ; and almost simultaneously with the advent of Hsien Fêng to the Imperial power, the long-smouldering discontent with Manchu rule, carefully fostered by the organization of the Triad

Society, broke into open rebellion. A sort of holy war was proclaimed against the Manchus, stigmatized as usurpers and idolaters, who were to be displaced by a native administration, called the T'ai P'ing (great peace) Heavenly Dynasty, at the head of which Hung placed himself, with the title of "Heavenly King," in allusion to the Christian principles on which this new departure was founded.

"Our Heavenly King," so ran the rebel proclamations, "has received a divine commission to exterminate the Manchus utterly, men, women, and children, with all idolaters, and to possess the empire as its true sovereign. For the empire and everything in it is his ; its mountains and rivers, its broad lands and public treasuries ; you and all that you have, your family, males and females alike, from yourself to your youngest child, and your property, from your patrimonial estates to the bracelet on your infant's arm. We command the services of all, and we take everything. All who resist us are rebels and idolatrous demons, and we kill them without sparing ; but whoever acknowledges our Heavenly King and exerts himself in our service shall have full reward,— due honour and station in the armies and court of the Heavenly Dynasty."

The T'ai-p'ings now got rid of the chief outward sign of allegiance to the Manchus, by ceasing to shave the forepart of the head, and allowing all their hair to grow long, from which they were often spoken of at the time—and the name still survives—as the long-haired rebels. Their early successes were phenomenal ; they captured city after city, moving northwards through Kuangsi into Hunan, whence, after a severe check at Ch'ang-sha, the provincial capital, the siege of which they were forced to raise, they reached and captured, among others, the important cities of Wu-ch'ang, Kiukiang, and An-ch'ing, on the Yangtsze. The next stage was to Nanking, a city occupying an important strategic position, and famous as the capital of the empire in the fourth and fourteenth centuries. Here the Manchu garrison offered but a feeble resistance, the only troops who fought at all being Chinese ; within ten days (March, 1853) the city was in the hands of the T'ai-p'ings ; all Manchus,—men, women, and children, said to number no fewer than twenty thousand,—were put to the sword ; and in the same month, Hung was formally proclaimed first Emperor of the T'ai P'ing Heavenly Dynasty, Nanking from this date receiving the name of the Heavenly City. So far, the generals who had been sent to oppose his progress had effected nothing. One of these was Commissioner Lin, of opium fame, who had been banished and recalled, and was then living in retirement after having successfully held several high offices. His health was not equal to the effort, and he died on his way to take up his post.

After the further capture of Chinkiang, a feat which created a considerable panic at Shanghai, a force was detached from the main body of the T'aip'ings, and dispatched north for no less a purpose than the capture of Peking. Apparently a foolhardy project, it was one that came nearer to realization than the most sanguine outsider could possibly have suspected. The army reached Tientsin, which is only eighty miles from the capital; but when there, a slight reverse, together with other unexplained reasons, resulted in a return (1855) of the troops without having accomplished their object. Meanwhile, the comparative ease with which the T'aip'ings had set the Manchus at defiance, and continued to hold their own, encouraged various outbreaks in other parts of the empire; until at length more systematic efforts were made to put a stop to the present impossible condition of affairs.

Opportunity just now was rather on the side of the Imperialists, as the futile expedition to Peking had left the rebels in a somewhat aimless state, not quite knowing what to do next. It is true that they were busy spreading the T'ai-p'ing conception of Christianity, in establishing schools, and preparing an educational literature to meet the exigencies of the time. They achieved the latter object by building

anew on the lines, but not in the spirit, of the old.
Thus, the Trimetrical Classic, the famous schoolboy's
handbook, a veritable guide to knowledge in which a
variety of subjects are lightly touched upon, was
entirely rewritten. The form, rhyming stanzas
with three words to each line, was preserved ; but
instead of beginning with the familiar Confucian
dogma that man's nature is entirely good at his
birth and only becomes depraved by later environ-
ment, we find the story of the Creation, taken from
the first chapter of Genesis.

By 1857, Imperialist troops were drawing close
lines around the rebels, who had begun to lose rather
than to gain ground. An-ch'ing and Nanking, the
only two cities which remained to them, were blockaded, and the Manchu plan was simply to starve
the enemy out. During this period we hear little of
the Emperor, Hsien Fêng ; and what we do hear is
not to his advantage. He had become a confirmed
debauchee, in the hands of a degraded clique, whose
only contribution to the crisis was a suggested issue
of paper money and debasement of the popular
coinage. Among his generals, however, there was
now one, whose name is still a household word all
over the empire, and who initiated the first checks
which led to the ultimate suppression of the rebellion.
Tsêng Kuo-fan had been already employed in high
offices, when, in 1853, he was first ordered to take up

arms against the Tʻai-pʻings. After some reverses, he entered upon a long course of victories by which the rebels were driven from most of their strongholds ; and in 1859, he submitted a plan for an advance on Nanking, which was approved and ultimately carried out. Meanwhile, the plight of the besieged rebels in Nanking had become so unbearable that something had to be done. A sortie on a large scale was accordingly organized, and so successful was it that the Tʻai-pʻings not only routed the besieging army, but were able to regain large tracts of territory, capturing at the same time huge stores of arms and munitions of war. These victories were in reality the death-blow to the rebel cause, for the brutal cruelty then displayed towards the unfortunate people at large was of such a character as to alienate completely the sympathy of thousands who might otherwise have been glad to see the end of the Manchus. Among other acts of desolation, the large and beautiful city of Soochow was burnt and looted, an outrage for which the Tʻai-pʻings were held responsible, and regarding which there is a pathetic tale told by an eye-witness of the ruins ; in this instance, however, if indeed in no others, the acts of vandalism in question were committed by Imperialist soldiers.

It is with the Tʻai-pʻing rebellion that we associate *likin*, a tax which has for years past been the bugbear of the foreign merchant in China. The term means " thousandth-part money," that is, the thousandth part of a *tael* or Chinese ounce of silver, say one *cash* ; and it was originally applied to a tax of one *cash* per tael on all sales, said to have been voluntarily imposed on themselves by the people, as a temporary measure, with a view to make up the deficiency in the land-tax caused by the rebellion. It was to be set apart for military purposes only— hence its common name " war-tax " ; but it soon drifted into the general body of taxation, and became a serious impost on foreign trade. We first hear of it in 1852, as collected by the Governor of Shantung ; to hear the last of it has long been the dream of those who wish to see the expansion of trade with China.

Tsêng Kuo-fan was now (1860) appointed Imperial War Commissioner as well as Viceroy of the Two Kiang (= provinces of Kiangsi and Kiangsu + Anhui). He had already been made a *baturu*, a kind of order instituted by the first Manchu Emperor, Shun Chih, as a reward for military prowess ; and had also received the Yellow Riding Jacket from the Emperor Hsien Fêng, who drew off the jacket he was himself wearing at the time, and placed it on the shoulders of his loyal and successful general. In 1861 he succeeded in recapturing An-ch'ing and other places ; and with this city

as his headquarters, siege was forthwith laid to
Nanking.

The Imperialist forces were at this juncture
greatly strengthened by the appointment, on Tsêng's
recommendation, of two notable men, Tso Tsung-
t'ang and Li Hung-chang, as Governors of Chehkiang
and Kiangsu respectively. Assistance, too, came
from another and most unexpected quarter. An
American adventurer, named Ward, a man of considerable military ability, organized a small force
of foreigners, which he led to such purpose against
the T'ai-p'ings, that he rapidly gathered into its
ranks a large if motley crowd of foreigners and
Chinese, all equally bent upon plunder, and with that
end in view submitting to the discipline necessary
to success. A long run of victories gained for this
force the title of the Ever Victorious Army ; until at
length Ward was killed in battle. He was buried
at Sungkiang, near Shanghai, a city which he had
retaken from the T'ai-p'ings, and there a shrine was
erected to his memory, and for a long time—perhaps
even now—offerings were made to his departed
spirit. An attempt was made to replace him by
another American named Burgevine, who had been
Ward's second in command. This man, however,
was found to be incapable and was superseded ; and
in 1863 Major Gordon, R.E., was allowed by the
British authorities to take over command of what

was then an army of about five thousand men, and to act in co-operation with Tsêng Kuo-fan and Li Hung-chang. Burgevine shortly afterwards went over to the rebels with about three hundred men, and finally came to a tragic end.

Gordon's appointment to the work which will always be associated with his name, was speedily followed by disastrous results to the T῾ai-p῾ings. The Ever Victorious troops, who had recently been worsted in more than one encounter with their now desperate enemies, began to retrieve their reputation, greatly stimulated by the regular pay which Gordon always insisted upon. Towards the close of the year, the siege of Soochow ended in a capitulation on terms which Gordon understood to include a pardon for the eight T῾ai-p῾ing " princes " engaged in its defence. These eight were hurriedly decapitated by order of Li Hung-chang, and Gordon immediately resigned, after having searched that same night, so the story goes, revolver in hand, for Li Hung-chang, whose brains he had determined to blow out on the spot. The Emperor sent him a medal and a present of about £3,000, both of which he declined ; and Imperial affairs would again have been in a bad way, but that Gordon, yielding to a sense of duty, agreed to resume command. Foreign interests had begun to suffer badly ; trade was paralysed ; and something had to be done. Further successes under

Gordon's leadership reduced the T'ai-p'ings to their last extremity. Only Nanking remained to be captured, and that was already fully invested by Tsêng Kuo-fan. Gordon therefore laid down his command, and was rewarded with the title of Provincial Commander-in-Chief, and also with the bestowal of the Yellow Riding Jacket. A month or so later (July, 1864), Nanking was carried by storm, defended bravely to the last by the only remaining "prince," the Heavenly King himself having taken poison three weeks beforehand. This prince escaped with the new king, a boy of sixteen, who had just succeeded his father ; but he was soon caught and executed, having first been allowed time to write a short history of the movement from the T'ai-p'ing point of view. The boy shared his fate. The Imperial edicts of this date show clearly what a sense of relief came over the Manchu court when once it could be said definitively that the great rebellion was over. On the other hand, there were not wanting some foreigners who would have liked to see the Manchus overthrown, and who severely blamed the British Government for helping to bolster up a dynasty already in the last stage of decay ; for it seems to be an indubitable fact that but for British intervention, the rebellion would ultimately have succeeded in that particular direction.

During a great part of the last eight years described above, an ordinary observer would have said that the Manchus had already sufficient troubles on hand, and would be slow to provoke further causes of anxiety. It is none the less true, however, that at one of the most critical periods of the rebellion, China was actually at war with the very power which ultimately came to the rescue. In 1856 the Viceroy of Canton, known to foreigners as Governor Yeh, a man who had gained favour at the Manchu court by his wholesale butchery of real and suspected rebels, arrested twelve Chinese sailors on board the " Arrow," a Chinese-owned vessel lying at Canton, which had been licensed at Hongkong to sail under the British flag, and at the same time the flag was hauled down by Yeh's men. Had this been an isolated act, it is difficult to see why very grave consequences need have followed, and perhaps Justin M'Carthy's condemnation of our Consul, Mr (afterwards Sir Harry) Parkes, as " fussy," because he sent at once to Hongkong for armed assistance, might in such case be allowed to stand unchallenged ; but it must be remembered that Yeh was all the time refusing to foreigners rights which had been already conceded under treaty, and that action such as Parkes took, against an adversary such as Yeh, was absolutely necessary either to mend or end the situation. Accordingly, his action led to what was at first an awkward state of reprisals, in

which some American men-of-war joined for grievances of their own; forts being attacked and
occupied, the foreign houses of business at Canton
being burned down, and rewards offered for
foreigners' heads. In January, 1857, an attempt
was actually made in Hongkong to get rid of all
foreigners at one fell stroke, in which plot there is
no doubt that the local officials at Canton were
deeply implicated. The bread was one day found
to be poisoned with arsenic, but so heavily that little
mischief was done. The only possible end to this
tension was war; and by the end of the year a joint
British and French force, with Lord Elgin and Baron
Gros as plenipotentiaries, was on the spot. Canton
was captured after a poor resistance; and Governor
Yeh, whose enormous bulk made escape difficult,
was captured and banished to Calcutta, where he
died. On the voyage he sank into a kind of stupor,
taking no interest whatever in his new surroundings;
and when asked by Alabaster, who accompanied
him as interpreter, why he did not read, he pointed
to his stomach, the Chinese receptacle for learning,
and said that there was nothing worth reading
except the Confucian Canon, and that he had already
got all that inside him. After his departure the
government of the city was successfully directed by
British and French authorities, acting in concert
with two high Manchu officials.

Lord Elgin then decided to proceed north, in the hope of being able to make satisfactory arrangements for future intercourse ; but the obstructive policy of the officials on his arrival at the Peiho compelled him to attack and capture the Taku forts, and finally, to take up his residence in Tientsin. The lips, as the Chinese say, being now gone, the teeth began to feel cold ; the court was in a state of panic, and within a few weeks a treaty was signed (June 26, 1858) containing, among other concessions to England, the right to have a diplomatic representative stationed in Peking, and permission to trade in the interior of China. It would naturally be supposed that Lord Elgin's mission was now ended, and indeed he went home ; the Emperor, however, would not hear of ratifications of the treaty being exchanged in Peking, and in many other ways it was made plain that there was no intention of its stipulations being carried out. There was the example of Confucius, who had been captured by rebels and released on condition that he would not travel to the State of Wei. Thither, not-withstanding, he continued his route ; and when asked by a disciple if it was right to violate his oath, he replied, " This was a forced oath ; the spirits do not hear such."

By June, 1859, another Anglo-French force was at the mouth of the Peiho, only to find the Taku forts now strongly fortified, and the river staked

and otherwise obstructed. The allied fleet, after
suffering considerable damage, with much loss of
life, was compelled to retire, greatly to the joy and
relief of the Emperor, who at last saw the barbarian
reduced to his proper status. It was on this occasion
that Commander Tatnell of the U.S. navy, who was
present, strictly speaking, as a spectator only, in
complete violation of international law, of which
luckily the Chinese knew nothing at that date, lent
efficient aid by towing boat-loads of British marines
into action, justifying his conduct by a saying which
will always be gratefully associated with his name,—
" Blood is thicker than water."

By August, 1860, thirteen thousand British troops,
seven thousand French, and two thousand five
hundred Cantonese coolies, were ready to make
another attempt. This time there were no frontal
attacks on the forts from the seaward ; capture was
effected, after a severe struggle, by land from the
rear, a feat which was generally regarded by the
Tartar soldiery as most unsportsmanlike. High
Manchu officials were now hurriedly dispatched
from Peking to Tientsin to stop by fair promises
the further advance of the allies ; but the British
and French plenipotentiaries decided to move up to
T'ung-chow, a dozen miles or so from the capital.
It was on this march that Parkes, Loch, and others,
while carrying out orders under a flag of truce,

were treacherously seized by the soldiers of Sêng-ko-lin-sin, the Manchu prince and general (familiar to the British troops as " Sam Collinson "), who had just experienced a severe defeat at the taking of the Taku forts. After being treated with every indignity, the prisoners, French and English, numbering over thirty in all, were forwarded to Peking. There they were miserably tortured, and many of them succumbed ; but events were moving quickly now, and relief was at hand for those for whom it was not already too late. Sêng-ko-lin-sin and his vaunted Tartar cavalry were completely routed in several encounters, and Peking lay at the mercy of the foreigner, the Emperor having fled to Jehol, where he died in less than a year. Only then did Prince Kung, a younger brother of Hsien Fêng, who had been left to bear the brunt of foreign resentment, send back, in a state too terrible for words, fourteen prisoners, less than half the original number of those so recently captured. Something in the form of a punitive act now became necessary, to mark the horror with which this atrocious treatment of prisoners by the Manchu court was regarded among the countrymen of the victims. Accordingly, orders were given to burn down the Summer Palace, appropriately condemned as being the favourite residence of the Emperor, and also the scene of the unspeakable tortures inflicted. This palace was surrounded by a beautiful pleasance lying on the slope of the western hills, about nine miles to the north-west of Peking. Yüan-ming Yüan, or the " Bright Round Garden," to give it its proper name, had been laid out by the Jesuit fathers on the plan of the Trianon at Versailles, and was packed with valuable porcelain, old bronzes, and every conceivable kind of curio, most of which were looted or destroyed by the infuriated soldiery.

The ratification of the Treaty of Tientsin (1858) was now completed, and before the end of the year the allied forces were gone, save and except garrisons at Tientsin and Taku, which were to remain until the indemnity was paid.

G

CHAPTER IX

T'UNG CHIH

ON the death of the Emperor, a plot was concocted by eight members of the extreme anti-foreign party at Court, who claimed to have been appointed Regents, to make away with the Empress Dowager, the concubine mother, known as the Western Empress, of the five-year-old child just proclaimed under the title of Chi Hsiang (good omen), and also the late Emperor's three brothers, thus securing to themselves complete control of the administration. Prince Kung, however, managed to be " first at the fire," and in accordance with the Chinese proverb, was therefore " first with his cooking." Having got wind of the scheme, in concert with the two Empresses Dowager, who had secured possession of the Emperor, he promptly caused the conspirators to be seized. Two of them, Imperial princes, were allowed to commit suicide, and the others were either executed or banished, while Prince Kung and the two Empresses formed a joint regency for the direction of public affairs, after changing the style of the reign from Chi Hsiang to T'ung Chih (united rule).

The position of these two Empresses was a curious

one. The Empress Dowager *par excellence*—for there is only one legal wife in China—had no children ; a concubine had provided the heir to the throne, and had in consequence been raised to the rank of Western Empress, subordinate only to the childless Eastern Empress. Of the latter, there is nothing to be said, except that she remained a cipher to the end of her life ; of the concubine, a great deal has been said, much of which is untrue. Taken from an ordinary Manchu family into the palace, she soon gained an extraordinary influence over Hsien Fêng, and began to make her voice heard in affairs of State. Always on the side of determined measures, she had counselled the Emperor to remain in Peking and face the barbarians ; she is further believed to have urged the execution of Parkes and Loch, the order luckily arriving too late to be carried out. For the next three years the Regents looked anxiously for the final collapse of the T'ai-p'ings, having meanwhile to put up with the hateful presence of foreign diplomats, now firmly established within the Manchu section of the city of Peking. No sooner was the great rebellion entirely suppressed (1864), than another rising broke out. The Nien-fei, or Twist Rebels, said to have been so called because they wore as a badge turbans twisted with grease, were mounted banditti who, here to-day and gone to-morrow, for several years

committed much havoc in the northern provinces of
China, until finally suppressed by Tso Tsung-t'ang.

Turkestan was the next part of the empire to claim
attention. A son and successor of Jehangir, ruling
as vassal of China at Khokand, had been murdered
by his lieutenant, Yakoob Beg, who, in 1866, had
set himself up as Ameer of Kashgaria, throwing off
the Manchu yoke and attracting to his standard
large numbers of discontented Mahometans from
all quarters. His attack upon the Dunganis, who
had risen on their own account and had spread
rebellion far and wide between the province of
Shensi and Kuldja, caused Russia to step in and
annex Kuldja before it could fall into his hands.
Still, he became master of a huge territory ; and in
1874 the title of Athalik Ghazi, " Champion Father,"
was conferred upon him by the Ameer of Bokhara.
He is also spoken of as the Andijani, from Andijan,
a town in Khokand whence he and many of his
followers came. Luckily for the Manchus, they
were able to avail themselves of the services of a
Chinese general whose extraordinary campaign on
this occasion has marked him as a commander of the
first order. Tso Tsung-t'ang, already distinguished
by his successes against the T'ai-p'ings and the
Nien-fei, began by operations, in 1869, against the
Mahometans in Shensi. Fighting his way through
difficulties caused by local outbreaks and mutinies

in his rear, he had captured by 1873 the important city of Su-chow in Kansuh, and by 1874 his advance-guard had reached Hami. There he was forced to settle down and raise a crop in order to feed his troops, supplies being very uncertain. In 1876 Urumtsi was recovered; and in 1877 Turfan, Harashar, Yarkand, and Kashgar. At this juncture, Yakoob Beg was assassinated, after having held Kashgaria for twelve years. Khoten fell on January 2, 1878. This wonderful campaign was now over, but China had lost Kuldja. A Manchu official, named Ch'ung-hou, who was sent to St Petersburg to meet Russian diplomats on their own ground, the main object being to recover this lost territory, was condemned to death on his return for the egregious treaty he had managed to negotiate, and was only spared at the express request of Queen Victoria; he will be mentioned again shortly. His error was afterwards retrieved by a young and brilliant official, son of the great Tsêng Kuo-fan, and later a familiar figure as the Marquis Tsêng, Minister at the Court of St James's, by whom Kuldja was added once more to the Manchu empire.

The year 1868 is remarkable for a singular episode. The Regents and other high authorities in Peking decided, at whose instigation can only be surmised, to send an embassy to the various countries of Europe and America, in order to bring to the notice of foreign governments China's right, as an independent Power, to manage her internal affairs without undue interference from outside. The mission, which included two Chinese officials, was placed under the leadership of Mr Burlingame, American Minister at Peking, who, in one of his speeches, took occasion to say that China was simply longing to cement friendly relations with foreign powers, and that within some few short years there would be " a shining cross on every hill in the Middle Kingdom."

Burlingame died early in 1870, before his mission was completed, and only four months before the Tientsin Massacre threw a shadow of doubt over his optimistic pronouncements. The native population at Tientsin had been for some time irritated by the height to which, contrary to their own custom, the towers of the Roman Catholic Cathedral had been carried ; and rumours had also been circulated that behind the lofty walls and dark mysterious portals of the Catholic foundling hospital, children's eyes and hearts were extracted from still warm corpses to furnish medicines for the barbarian pharmacopœia. On June 21, the cathedral and the establishment of sisters of mercy, the French Consulate and other buildings, were pillaged and burnt by a mob composed partly of the rowdies of the place and partly of soldiers who happened to be temporarily quartered there. All the priests and sisters were brutally murdered, as also the French Consul and other foreigners. For this outrage eighteen men were executed, a large indemnity was exacted, and the superintendent of trade, the same Manchu official whose subsequent diplomatic failure at St Petersburg has been already noticed, was sent to France with a letter of apology from the Emperor.

In 1872 T'ung Chih was married, and in the following year took over the reins of government. Thereupon, the foreign Ministers pressed for personal interviews ; and after much obstruction on the part of the Manchu court, the first audience was granted. This same year saw the collapse of the Panthays, a tribe of Mahometans in Yünnan who, so far back as 1855, had begun to free themselves from Chinese rule. They chose as their leader an able co-religionist named Tu Wên-hsiu, who was styled Sultan Sulei-man, and he sent agents to Burma to buy arms and munitions of war ; after which, secure in the natural fortress of Ta-li, he was soon master of all western Yünnan. In 1863 he repulsed with heavy loss two armies sent against him from the provincial capital ; but the end of the T'ai-p'ing rebellion set free the whole resources of the empire against him, and he remained inactive while the Imperialists advanced leisurely westwards. In 1871 he tried vainly to obtain aid from England, sending over his son, Prince Hassan, for that purpose. The following year saw the enemy at the gates of Ta-li, and by and by there was a treacherous surrender of an important position. Then a promise of an amnesty was obtained at the price of Tu's head, and an enormous indemnity. On January 15, 1873, his family having all committed suicide, the Sultan passed for the last time through the crowded streets of Ta-li on his way to the camp of his victorious adversary. He arrived there senseless, having taken poison before setting forth. His corpse was beheaded and his head was forwarded to the provincial capital, and thence in a jar of honey to Peking.

His conqueror, whose name is not worth recording, was one of those comparatively rare Chinese monsters who served their Manchu masters only too well. Eleven days after the Sultan's death, he invited the chief men of the town to a feast, and after putting them all to death, gave the signal for a general massacre, in which thirty thousand persons are said to have been butchered.

In 1874 the Japanese appear on the scene, adding fresh troubles to those with which the Manchus were already encompassed. Some sailors from the Loochoo Islands, over which Japanese sovereignty had been successfully maintained, were murdered by the savages on the east coast of Formosa ; and

failing to obtain redress, Japan sent a punitive
expedition to the island, and began operations
on her own account, but withdrew on promises
of amendment and payment of all expenses
incurred.

CHAPTER X

In 1875 the Emperor T'ung Chih died of smallpox, and with his death the malign influence of his mother comes more freely into play. The young Empress was about to become a mother ; and had she borne a son, her position as mother of the baby Emperor would have been of paramount importance, while the grandmother, the older Empress Dowager, would have been relegated to a subordinate status. Consequently,—it may now be said, having regard to subsequent happenings,—the death of the Empress followed that of her husband at an indecently short interval, for no particular reason of health ; and the old Empress Dowager became supreme. In order to ensure her supremacy, she had previously, on the very day of the Emperor's death, caused the succession to be allotted, in utter violation of established custom, to a first cousin, making him heir to the Emperor Hsien Fêng, instead of naming one of a lower generation who, as heir to T'ung Chih, would have been qualified to sacrifice to the spirit of his adopted father. Thus, the late Emperor was left without a son, and his spirit without a ministrant

at ancestral worship, the only consolation being that
when a son should be born to the new Emperor (aged
four), that child was to become son by adoption to
his late Majesty, T'ung Chih. Remonstrances, even
from Manchus, were soon heard on all sides ; but to
these the Empress Dowager paid no attention until
four years afterwards (1879), on the occasion of
the deferred funeral of the late Emperor, when a
censor, named Wu K'o-tu, committed suicide at
the mausoleum, leaving behind him a memorial in
which he strongly condemned the action of the two
Empresses Dowager, still regarded officially as joint
regents, and called for a re-arrangement of the
succession, under which the late Emperor would
be duly provided with an heir. Nothing, however,
came of this sacrifice, except promises, until 1900.
A son of Prince Tuan, within a few months to
espouse the Boxer cause, was then made heir to his
late Majesty, as required ; but at the beginning of
1901, this appointment was cancelled and the spirit
of the Emperor T'ung Chih was left once more
unprovided for in the ancestral temple. The first
cousin in question, who reigned as Kuang Hsü
(=brilliant succession), was not even the next
heir in his own generation ; but he was a child of
four, and that suited the plans of the Empress
Dowager, who, having appointed herself Regent, now
entered openly upon the career for which she will be

remembered in history. What she would have done if the Empress had escaped and given birth to a son, can only be a matter of conjecture.

In 1876 the first resident Envoy ever sent by China to Great Britain, or to any other nation, was accredited to the Court of St James's. Kuo Sung-tao, who was chosen for the post, was a fine scholar ; he made several attempts on the score of health to avoid what then seemed to all Chinese officials— no Manchu would have been sent—to be a dangerous and unpleasant duty, but was ultimately obliged to proceed. It was he who, on his departure in 1879, said to Lord Salisbury that he liked everything about the English very much, except their shocking immorality.

The question of railways for China had long been simmering in the minds of enterprising foreigners ; but it was out of the question to think that the Government would allow land to be sold for such a purpose ; therefore there would be no sellers. In 1876 a private company succeeded in obtaining the necessary land by buying up connecting strips between Shanghai and Woosung at the mouth of the river, about eight miles in all. The company then proceeded to lay down a miniature railway, which was an object of much interest to the native, whose amusement soon took the form of a trip there and back. Political influence was then brought to bear, and the whole thing was purchased by the Government ; the rails were torn up and sent to Formosa, where they were left to rot upon the sea-beach.

The suppression of rebellion in Turkestan and Yünnan has already been mentioned ; also the retrocession of Kuldja, which brings us down to the year 1881, when the Eastern Empress died. Death must have been more or less a relief to this colourless personage, who had been entirely superseded on a stage on which by rights she should have played the leading part, and who had been terrorized during her last years by her more masterful colleague.

In 1882 there were difficulties with France over Tongking ; these, however, were adjusted, and in 1884 a convention was signed by Captain Fournier and Li Hung-chang. A further dispute then arose as to a breach of the convention by the Chinese, and an *état de représailles* followed, during which the French destroyed the Chinese fleet. After the peace which was arranged in 1885, a few years of comparative tranquillity ensued ; the Emperor was married (1889), and relieved his aunt of her duties as Regent.

Japan, in earlier centuries contemptuously styled the Dwarf-nation, and always despised as a mere imitator and brain-picker of Chinese wisdom, now swims definitively into the ken of the Manchu court. The Formosan imbroglio had been forgotten as soon as it was over, and the recent rapid progress of Japan

on Western lines towards national strength had been
ignored by all Manchu statesmen, each of whom lived
in hope that the deluge would not come in his own
time. So far back as 1885, in consequence of serious
troubles involving much bloodshed, the two countries
had agreed that neither should send troops to Korea
without due notification to the other. Now, in
1894, China violated this contract by dispatching
troops, at the request of the king of Korea, whose
throne was threatened by a serious rebellion, without
sufficient warning to Japan, and further, by keeping
a body of these troops at the Korean capital even
when the rebellion was at an end. A disastrous
war ensued. The Japanese were victorious on land
and sea ; the Chinese fleet was destroyed ; Port
Arthur was taken ; and finally, after surrendering
Wei-hai-wei (1895), to which he had retired with the
remnant of his fleet, Admiral Ting, well known as
" a gallant sailor and true gentleman," committed
suicide together with four of his captains. Li Hung-
chang was then sent to Japan to sue for peace, and
while there he was shot in the cheek by a fanatical
member of the Soshi class. This act brought him
much sympathy—he was then seventy-two years
old ; and in the treaty of Shimonoseki, which he
negotiated, better terms perhaps were obtained
than would otherwise have been the case. The
terms granted included the independence of Korea,

for centuries a tribute-paying vassal of China, and the cession of the island of Formosa. Japan had occupied the peninsula on which stands the impregnable fortress of Port Arthur, and had captured the latter in a few hours ; but she was not to be allowed to keep them. A coalition of European powers, Russia, Germany, and France—England refused to join—decided that it would never do to let Japan possess Port Arthur, and forced her to accept a money payment instead. So it was restored to China—for the moment ; and at the same time a republic was declared in Formosa ; but of this the Japanese made short work.

The following year was marked by an unusual display of initiative on the part of the Emperor, who now ordered the introduction of railways ; but in 1897 complications with foreign powers rather gave a check to these aspirations. Two German Catholic priests were murdered, and as a punitive measure Germany seized Kiaochow in Shantung ; while in 1898 Russia " leased " Port Arthur, and as a counterblast England thought it advisable to " lease " Wei-hai-wei. So soon as the Manchu court had recovered from the shock of these events, and had resumed its normal state of torpor, it was rudely shaken from within by a series of edicts which peremptorily commanded certain reforms of a most far-reaching description. For instance, the great public examinations, which had been conducted on much the same system for seven or eight centuries past, were to be modified by the introduction of subjects suggested by recent intercourse with Western nations. There was to be a university in Peking, and the temples, which cover the empire in all directions, were to be closed to religious services and opened for educational purposes. The Manchus, indeed, have never shown any signs of a religious temperament. There had not been, under the dynasty in question, any such wave of devotional fervour as was experienced under more than one previous dynasty. Neither the dreams of Buddhism, nor the promises of immortality held out by the Taoist, seem to have influenced in a religious, as opposed to a superstitious sense, the rather Bœotian mind of the Manchu. The learned emperors of the seventeenth and eighteenth centuries accepted Confucianism as sufficient for every-day humanity, and did all in their power to preserve it as a quasi-State religion. Thus, Buddhism was not favoured at the expense of Taoism, nor *vice versa* ; Mahometanism was tolerated so long as there was no suspicion of disloyalty ; Christianity, on the other hand, was bitterly opposed, being genuinely regarded for a long time as a cloak for territorial aggression.

To return to the reforms. Young Manchus of noble family were to be sent abroad for an education

on wider lines than it was possible to obtain at home.
This last was in every way a desirable measure.
No Manchu had ever visited the West; all the
officials previously sent to foreign countries had
been Chinese. But other proposed changes were not
of equal value.

At the back of this reform movement was a small
band of earnest men who suffered from too much
zeal, which led to premature action. A plot was
conceived, under which the Empress Dowager was
to be arrested and imprisoned; but this was betrayed by Yüan Shih-k'ai, and she turned the tables
by suddenly arresting and imprisoning the Emperor,
and promptly decapitating all the conspirators,
with the exception of K'ang Yu-wei, who succeeded
in escaping. He had been the moving spirit of this
abortive revolution; he was a fine scholar, and had
completely gained the ear of the Emperor. The
latter became henceforth to the end of his life a
person of no importance, while China, for the third
time in history, passed under the dominion of a
woman. There was no secret about it; the Empress
Dowager, popularly known as the Old Buddha, had
succeeded in terrorizing every one who came into
contact with her, and her word was law. It was
said of one of the Imperial princes that he was
" horribly afraid of her Majesty, and that when she
spoke to him he was on tenter-hooks, as though

H

thorns pricked him, and the sweat ran down his face."

All promise of reform now disappeared from the Imperial programme, and the recent edicts, which had raised premature hope in this direction, were annulled ; the old régime was to prevail once more. The weakness of this policy was emphasized in the following year (1899), when England removed from Japan the stigma of extra-territorial jurisdiction, by which act British defendants, in civil and criminal cases alike, now became amenable to Japanese tribunals.   Japan had set herself to work to frame a code, and had trained lawyers for the administration of justice ; China had done nothing, content that on her own territory foreigners and their lawsuits, as above, should be tried by foreign Consuls.   One curious edict of this date had for its object the conferment of duly graded civil rank, the right to salutes at official visits, and similar ceremonial privileges, upon Roman Catholic archbishops, bishops, and priests of the missionary body in China.   The Catholic view was that the missionaries would gain in the eyes of the people if treated with more deference than the majority of Chinese officials cared to display towards what was to them an objectionable class ; in practice, however, the system was found to be unworkable, and was ultimately given up.

The autumn of this year witnessed the beginning

of the so-called Boxer troubles. There was great unrest, especially in Shantung, due, it was said, to ill-feeling between the people at large and converts to Christianity, and at any rate aggravated by recent foreign acquisitions of Chinese territory. It was thus that what was originally one of the periodical anti-dynastic risings, with the usual scion of the Ming dynasty as figure-head, lost sight of its objective and became a bloodthirsty anti-foreign outbreak. The story of the siege of the Legations has been written from many points of view ; and most people know all they want to know of the two summer months in 1900, the merciless bombardment of a thousand foreigners, with their women and children, cooped up in a narrow space, and also of the awful butchery of missionaries, men, women, and children alike, which took place at the capital of Shansi. Whatever may have been the origin of the movement, there can be little doubt that it was taken over by the Manchus, with the complicity of the Empress Dowager, as a means of getting rid of all the foreigners in China. Considering the extraordinary position the Empress Dowager had created for herself, it is impossible to believe that she would not have been able to put an end to the siege by a word, or even by a mere gesture. She did not do so ; and on the relief of the Legations, for a second time in her life—she had accompanied Hsien Fêng to

Jehol in 1860—she sought safety in an ignominious flight. Meanwhile, in response to a memorial from the Governor of Shansi, she had sent him a secret decree, saying, " Slay all foreigners wheresoever you find them ; even though they be prepared to leave your province, yet must they be slain." A second and more urgent decree said, " I command that all foreigners, men, women, and children, be summarily executed. Let not one escape, so that my empire may be purged of this noisome source of corruption, and that peace may be restored to my loyal subjects." The first of these decrees had been circulated to all the high provincial officials, and the result might well have been indiscriminate slaughter of foreigners all over China, but for the action of two Chinese officials, who had already incurred the displeasure of the Empress Dowager by memorializing against the Boxer policy. These men secretly changed the word " slay " into " protect," and this is the sense in which the decree was acted upon by provincial officials generally, with the exception of the Governor of Shansi, who sent a second memorial, eliciting the second decree as above. It is impossible to say how many foreigners owe their lives to this alteration of a word, and the Empress Dowager herself would scarcely have escaped so easily as she did, had her cruel order been more fully executed. The trick was soon discovered, and the two heroes, Yüan

Ch'ang and Hsü Ching-ch'êng, were both summarily beheaded, even although it was to the former that the Empress Dowager was indebted for information which enabled her to frustrate the plot against her life in 1898.

Now, at the very moment of departure, she perpetrated a most brutal crime. A favourite concubine of the Emperor's, who had previously given cause for offence, urged that his Majesty should not take part in the flight, but should remain in Peking. For this suggestion the Empress Dowager caused the miserable girl to be thrown down a well, in spite of the supplications of the Emperor on her behalf. Then she fled, ultimately to Hsi-an Fu, the capital of Shensi, and for a year and a half Peking was rid of her presence. In 1902, she came back with the Emperor, whose prerogative she still managed to usurp. She declared at once for reform, and took up the cause with much show of enthusiasm ; but those who knew the Manchu best, decided to " wait and see." She began by suggesting intermarriage between Manchus and Chinese, which had so far been prohibited, and advised Chinese women to give up the practice of footbinding, a custom which the ruling race had never adopted. It was henceforth to be lawful for Manchus, even of the Imperial family, to send their sons abroad to be educated,—a step which no Manchu would be likely to take unless forcibly coerced into doing so. Any spirit of enterprise which might have been possessed by the founders of the dynasty had long since evaporated, and all that Manchu nobles asked was to be allowed to batten in peace upon the Chinese people.

The direct issue of the emperors of the present dynasty and of their descendants in the male line, dating from 1616, are popularly known as Yellow Girdles, from a sash of that colour which they habitually wear. Each generation becomes a degree lower in rank, until they are mere members of the family with no rank whatever, although they still wear the girdle and receive a trifling allowance from the government. Thus, beggars and even thieves are occasionally seen with this badge of relationship to the throne. Members of the collateral branches of the Imperial family wear a red girdle, and are known as Gioros, Gioro being part of the surname—Aisin Gioro=Golden Race—of an early progenitor of the Manchu emperors.

As a next step in reform, the examination system was to be remodelled, but not in the one sense in which it would have appealed most to the Chinese people. Examinations for Manchus have always been held separately, and the standard attained has always been very far below that reached by Chinese candidates, so that the scholarship of the Manchu became long ago a by-word and a joke. Now, in

1904, it was settled that entry to an official career should be obtainable only through the modern educational colleges ; but this again applied only to Chinese and not to Manchus. The Manchus have always had wisdom enough to employ the best abilities they could discover by process of examination among the Chinese, many of whom have risen from the lowest estate to the highest positions in the empire, and have proved themselves valuable servants and staunch upholders of the dynasty. Still, in addition to numerous other posts, it may be said that all the fat sinecures have always been the portion of Manchus. For instance, the office of Hoppo, or superintendent of customs at Canton (abolished 1904), was a position which was allowed to degenerate into a mere opportunity for piling a large fortune in the shortest possible time, no particular ability being required from the holder of the post, who was always a Manchu.

Then followed a mission to Europe, at the head of which we now find a Manchu of high rank, an Imperial Duke, sent to study the mysteries of constitutional government, which was henceforth promised to the people, so soon as its introduction might be practicable. In the midst of these attractive promises (1904-5) came the Russo-Japanese war, with all its surprises. Among other causes to which the Manchu court ascribed the success of the Japanese, freedom from the opium vice took high rank, and this led to really serious enactments against the growth and consumption of opium in China. Continuous and strenuous efforts of philanthropists during the preceding half century had not produced any results at all; but now it seemed as though this weakness had been all along the chief reason for China's failures in her struggles with the barbarian, and it was to be incontinently stamped out. Ten years' grace was allowed, at the end of which period there was to be no more opium-smoking in the empire. One awkward feature was that the Empress Dowager herself was an opium-smoker; the difficulty, however, was got over by excluding from the application of the edict of 1906 persons over sixty years of age. Whatever may be thought of the wisdom of this policy, which so far has chiefly resulted in the substitution of morphia, cocaine, and alcohol, the thoroughness and rapidity with which it has been carried out, can only command the admiration of all; of those most who know China best.

CHAPTER XI

HSÜAN T'UNG

THE health of the Emperor, never very good, now began to fail, and by 1908 he was seriously ill ; in this same year, too, there were signs that the Empress Dowager was breaking up. Her last political act of any importance, except the nomination of the heir to the throne, was to issue a decree confirming the previous promise of constitutional government, which was to come into full force within nine years. Not many weeks later the Emperor died (November 14), the Empress Dowager having already, while he lay dying, appointed one of his nephews, a child barely three years old, to succeed him, in the vain hope that she would thus enjoy a further spell of power until the child should be of age. But on the following day the Empress Dowager also died ; a singular coincidence which has been attributed to the determination of the eunuchs and others that the Emperor should not outlive his aunt, for some time past seen to be "drawing near the wood," lest his reforming spirit should again jeopardize their nefarious interests.

The Regency devolved upon the Emperor's father,

but was not of very long duration. There was a show of introducing constitutional reform under the guise of provincial and national assemblies intended to control the government of the empire ; but after all, the final power to accept or reject their measures was vested in the Emperor, which really left things very much as they had been. The new charter was not found to be of much value, and there is little doubt that the Manchus regarded it in the light of what is known in China as a " dummy document," a measure to be extolled in theory, but not intended to appear in practice. Suddenly, in September 1911, the great revolution broke out, and the end came more rapidly than was expected.

It must not be imagined that this revolution was an inspiration of the moment ; on the contrary, it had been secretly brewing for quite a long time beforehand. During that period a few persons familiar with China may have felt that something was coming, but nobody knew exactly what. Those who accept without reservation the common state- ment that there is no concealment possible in a country where everybody is supposed to have his price, and that due notice of anything important is sure to leak out, must have been rather astonished when, without any warning, they found China in the throes of a well-planned revolution, which was over, with its object gained, almost as soon as the real gravity of the situation was realized. It is true that under the Manchus access to official papers of the most private description was always to be obtained at a moderate outlay ; it was thus, for instance, that we were able to appreciate the inmost feelings of that grim old Manchu, Wo-jen, who, in 1861, presented a secret memorial to the throne, and stated therein that his loathing of all foreigners was so great that he longed to eat their flesh and sleep on their skins.

The guiding spirit of the movement, Sun Yat-sen, is a native of Kuangtung, where he was born, not very far from Canton, in 1866. After some early education in Honolulu, he became a student at the College of Medicine, Hongkong, where he took his diploma in 1892. But his chief aim in life soon became a political one, and he determined to get rid of the Manchus. He organized a Young China party in Canton, and in 1895 made an attempt to seize the city. The plot failed, and fifteen out of the sixteen conspirators were arrested and executed ; Sun Yat-sen alone escaped. A year later, he was in London, preparing himself for further efforts by the study of Western forms of government, a very large reward being offered by the Chinese Government for his body, dead or alive. During his stay there he was decoyed into the Chinese Legation, and imprisoned in an upper room, from which he would have been hurried away to China, probably as a lunatic, to share the fate of his fifteen fellow-conspirators, but for the assistance of a woman who had been told off to wait upon him. To her he confided a note addressed to Dr Cantlie, a personal friend of long standing, under whom he had studied medicine in Hongkong; and she handed this to her husband, employed as waiter in the Legation, by whom it was safely delivered. He thus managed to communicate with the outer world; Lord Salisbury intervened, and he was released after a fortnight's detention.

Well might Sun Yat-sen now say—

> "They little thought that day of pain
> That one day I should come again."

More a revolutionary than ever, he soon set to work to collect funds, which flowed in freely from Chinese sources in all quarters of the world. At last, in September 1911, the train was fired, beginning with the province of Ssǔch'uan, and within an incredibly short space of time, half China was ablaze. By the middle of October the Manchus were beginning to feel that a great crisis was at hand, and the Regent was driven to recall Yüan Shih-k'ai, whom he had summarily dismissed from office two years before, on the conventional plea that Yüan was suffering from a bad leg, but really out of revenge for his treachery to the late Emperor, which had brought about the latter's arrest and practical deposition by the old Empress Dowager in 1898.

To this summons Yüan slily replied that he could not possibly leave home just then, as his leg was not yet well enough for him to be able to travel, meaning, of course, to gain time, and be in a position to dictate his own terms. On the 30th October, when it was already too late, the baby Emperor, reigning under the year-title Hsüan T'ung (wide control), published the following edict :—

" I have reigned for three years, and have always acted conscientiously in the interests of the people, but I have not employed men properly, not having political skill. I have employed too many nobles in political positions, which contravenes constitutionalism. On railway matters someone whom I trusted fooled me, and thus public opinion was opposed. When I urged reform, the officials and gentry seized the opportunity to embezzle. When old laws are abolished, high officials serve their own ends. Much of the people's money has been taken, but nothing to benefit the people has been achieved. On several occasions edicts have promulgated laws, but none of them have been obeyed. People are grumbling, yet I do not know; disasters loom ahead, but I do not see.

" The Ssŭch'uan trouble first occurred ; the Wuch'ang rebellion followed ; now alarming reports

come from Shansi and Hunan. In Canton and
Kiangsi riots appear. The whole empire is seething.
The minds of the people are perturbed. The spirits
of our nine late emperors are unable properly to
enjoy sacrifices, while it is feared the people will
suffer grievously.

"All these are my own fault, and hereby I
announce to the world that I swear to reform, and,
with our soldiers and people, to carry out the constitution faithfully, modifying legislation, developing the
interests of the people, and abolishing their hard-
ships—all in accordance with the wishes and interests
of the people. Old laws that are unsuitable will be
abolished."

Nowhere else in the world is the belief that Fortune
has a wheel which in the long run never fails to
"turn and lower the proud," so prevalent or so
deeply-rooted as in China. "To prosperity," says
the adage, "must succeed decay,"—a favourite
theme around which the novelist delights to weave
his romance. This may perhaps account for the
tame resistance of the Manchus to what they recognized as the inevitable.. They had enjoyed a
good span of power, quite as lengthy as that of any
dynasty of modern times, and now they felt that
their hour had struck. To borrow another phrase,
"they had come in with the roar of a tiger, to dis-
appear like the tail of a snake."

On November 3, certain regulations were issued by the National Assembly as the necessary basis upon which a constitution could be raised. The absolute veto of the Emperor was now withdrawn, and it was expressly stated that Imperial decrees were not to over-ride the law, though even here we find the addition of " except in the event of immediate necessity." The first clause of this document was confined to the following prophetic statement : " The Ta Ch'ing dynasty shall reign for ever."

On November 8, Yüan Shih-k'ai was appointed Prime Minister, and on December 3, the new Empress Dowager issued an edict, in which she said :

" The Regent has verbally memorialized the Empress Dowager, saying that he has held the Regency for three years, and his administration has been unpopular, and that constitutional government has not been consummated. Thus complications arose, and people's hearts were broken, and the country thrown into a state of turmoil. Hence one man's mismanagement has caused the nation to suffer miserably. He regrets his repentance is already too late, and feels that if he continues in power his commands will soon be disregarded. He wept and prayed to resign the regency, expressing the earnest intention of abstaining in the future from politics. I, the Empress Dowager, living within the palace, am ignorant of the state of affairs but I know that rebellion exists and fighting is continuing, causing disasters everywhere, while the commerce of friendly nations suffers. I must enquire into the circumstances and find a remedy. The Regent is honest, though ambitious and unskilled in politics. Being misled, he has harmed the people, and therefore his resignation is accepted. The Regent's seal is cancelled. Let the Regent receive fifty thousand *taels* annually from the Imperial household allowances, and hereafter the Premier and the Cabinet will control appointments and administration. Edicts are to be sealed with the Emperor's seal. I will lead the Emperor to conduct audiences. The guardianship of the holy person of the Emperor, who is of tender age, is a special responsibility. As the time is critical, the princes and nobles must observe the Ministers, who have undertaken a great responsibility, and be loyal and help the country and people, who now must realize that the Court does not object to the surrender of the power vested in the throne. Let the people preserve order and continue business, and thus prevent the country's disruption and restore prosperity."

CHAPTER XII

ON January 1, 1912, Sun Yat-sen entered the republican capital, Nanking, and received a salute of twenty-one guns. He assumed the presidency of the provisional government, swearing allegiance, and taking an oath to dethrone the Manchus, restore peace, and establish a government based upon the people's will. These objects accomplished, he was prepared to resign his office, thus enabling the people to elect a president of a united China. The first act of the provisional government was to proclaim a new calendar forthwith, January 1 becoming the New Year's Day of the republic.

On January 5 was issued the following republican manifesto :—

" To all friendly nations,—Greeting. Hitherto irremediable suppression of the individual qualities and the national aspirations of the people having arrested the intellectual, moral, and material development of China, the aid of revolution was invoked to extirpate the primary cause. We now proclaim the consequent overthrow of the despotic

I   129

sway of the Manchu dynasty, and the establishment of a republic. The substitution of a republic for a monarchy is not the fruit of transient passion, but the natural outcome of a long-cherished desire for freedom, contentment, and advancement. We Chinese people, peaceful and law-abiding, have not waged war except in self-defence. We have borne our grievance for two hundred and sixty-seven years with patience and forbearance. We have endeavoured by peaceful means to redress our wrongs, secure liberty, and ensure progress ; but we failed. Oppressed beyond human endurance, we deemed it our inalienable right, as well as a sacred duty, to appeal to arms to deliver ourselves and our posterity from the yoke to which we have for so long been subjected. For the first time in history an inglorious bondage is transformed into inspiring freedom. The policy of the Manchus has been one of unequivocal seclusion and unyielding tyranny. Beneath it we have bitterly suffered. Now we submit to the free peoples of the world the reasons justifying the revolution and the inauguration of the present government. Prior to the usurpation of the throne by the Manchus the land was open to foreign intercourse, and religious tolerance existed, as is shown by the writings of Marco Polo and the inscription on the Nestorian tablet at Hsi-an Fu. Dominated by ignorance and selfishness, the

Manchus closed the land to the outer world, and plunged the Chinese into a state of benighted mentality calculated to operate inversely to their natural talents, thus committing a crime against humanity and the civilized nations which it is almost impossible to expiate. Actuated by a desire for the perpetual subjugation of the Chinese, and a vicious craving for aggrandizement and wealth, the Manchus have governed the country to the lasting injury and detriment of the people, creating privileges and monopolies, erecting about themselves barriers of exclusion, national custom, and personal conduct, which have been rigorously maintained for centuries. They have levied irregular and hurtful taxes without the consent of the people, and have restricted foreign trade to treaty ports. They have placed the *likin* embargo on merchandise, obstructed internal commerce, retarded the creation of industrial enterprises, rendered impossible the development of natural resources, denied a regular system of impartial administration of justice, and inflicted cruel punishment on persons charged with offences, whether innocent or guilty. They have connived at official corruption, sold offices to the highest bidder, subordinated merit to influence, rejected the most reasonable demands for better government, and reluctantly conceded so-called reforms under the most urgent pressure, promising without any inten-

tion of fulfilling. They have failed to appreciate
the anguish-causing lessons taught them by foreign
Powers, and in process of years have brought themselves and our people beneath the contempt of the
world. A remedy of these evils will render possible
the entrance of China into the family of nations.
We have fought and have formed a government.
Lest our good intentions should be misunderstood,
we publicly and unreservedly declare the following
to be our promises :—

"The treaties entered into by the Manchus before
the date of the revolution, will be continually effective
to the time of their termination. Any and all
treaties entered into after the commencement of the
revolution will be repudiated. Foreign loans and
indemnities incurred by the Manchus before the
revolution will be acknowledged. Payments made
by loans incurred by the Manchus after its commencement will be repudiated. Concessions granted
to nations and their nationals before the revolution
will be respected. Any and all granted after it will
be repudiated. The persons and property of
foreign nationals within the jurisdiction of the
republic will be respected and protected. It will be
our constant aim and firm endeavour to build on a
stable and enduring foundation a national structure
compatible with the potentialities of our long-
neglected country. We shall strive to elevate the

people to secure peace and to legislate for prosperity. Manchus who abide peacefully in the limits of our jurisdiction will be accorded equality, and given protection.

" We will remodel the laws, revise the civil, criminal, commercial, and mining codes, reform the finances, abolish restrictions on trade and commerce, and ensure religious toleration and the cultivation of better relations with foreign peoples and governments than have ever been maintained before. It is our earnest hope that those foreign nations who have been steadfast in their sympathy will bind more firmly the bonds of friendship between us, and will bear in patience with us the period of trial confronting us and our reconstruction work, and will aid the consummation of the far-reaching plans, which we are about to undertake, and which they have long vainly been urging upon our people and our country.

" With this message of peace and good-will the republic cherishes the hope of being admitted into the family of nations, not merely to share its rights and privileges, but to co-operate in the great and noble task of building up the civilization of the world.

SUN YAT-SEN, *President.*"

The next step was to displace the three-cornered Dragon flag, itself of quite modern origin, in favour

of a new republican emblem. For this purpose
was designed a flag of five stripes,—yellow, red, blue,
white, black,—arranged at right angles to the flag-
staff in the above order, and intended to represent
the five races—Chinese, Manchus, Mongols, Tibetan,
Mussulmans—gathered together under one rule.

On February 12, three important edicts were
issued. In the first, the baby-emperor renounces the
throne, and approves the establishment of a provisional republican government, under the direction
of Yüan Shih-k'ai, in conjunction with the existing
provisional government at Nanking. In the second,
approval is given to the terms under which the
emperor retires, the chief item of which was an
annual grant of four million *taels*. Other more
sentimental privileges included the retention of a
bodyguard, and the continuance of sacrifices to the
spirits of the departed Manchu emperors. In the
third, the people are exhorted to preserve order
and abide by the Imperial will regarding the new
form of government.

Simultaneously with the publication of these
edicts, the last scene of the drama was enacted near
Nanking, at the mausoleum of the first sovereign of
the Ming dynasty (A.D. 1368-1644). Sun Yat-sen,
as provisional first president, accompanied by his
Cabinet and a numerous escort, proceeded thither,
and after offering sacrifice as usual, addressed,

through a secretary, the following oration to the
tablet representing the names of that great hero :—

" Of old the Sung dynasty became effete, and the
Kitan Tartars and Yüan dynasty Mongols seized the
occasion to throw this domain of China into confusion, to the fierce indignation of gods and men.
It was then that your Majesty, our founder, arose
in your wrath from obscurity, and destroyed those
monsters of iniquity, so that the ancient glory was
won again.   In twelve years you consolidated the
Imperial sway, and the dominions of the Great Yü
were purged of pollution and cleansed from the
noisome Tartar.   Often in history has our noble
Chinese race been enslaved by petty frontier barbarians from the north.   Never have such glorious
triumphs been won over them as your Majesty
achieved.   But your descendants were degenerate,
and failed to carry on your glorious heritage ; they
entrusted the reins of government to bad men, and
pursued a short-sighted policy.   In this way they
encouraged the ambitions of the eastern Tartar
savages (Manchus), and fostered the growth of their
power.   They were thus able to take advantage of
the presence of rebels to invade and possess themselves of your sacred capital.   From a bad eminence
of glory basely won, they lorded it over this most
holy soil, and our beloved China's rivers and hills

were defiled by their corrupting touch, while the
people fell victims to the headsman's axe or the
avenging sword. Although worthy patriots and
faithful subjects of your dynasty crossed the mountain ranges into Canton and the far south, in the hope
of redeeming the glorious Ming tradition from utter
ruin, and of prolonging a thread of the old dynasty's
life, although men gladly perished one after the other
in the forlorn attempt, heaven's wrath remained
unappeased, and mortal designs failed to achieve
success. A brief and melancholy page was added
to the history of your dynasty, and that was all.

" As time went on, the law became ever harsher, and
the meshes of its inexorable net grew closer. Alas
for our Chinese people, who crouched in corners and
listened with startled ears, deprived of power of
utterance, and with tongues glued to their mouths,
for their lives were past saving. Those others
usurped titles to fictitious clemency and justice,
while prostituting the sacred doctrines of the sages :
whom they affected to honour. They stifled public
opinion in the empire in order to force acquiescence
in their tyranny. The Manchu despotism became so
thorough and so embracing that they were enabled
to prolong their dynasty's existence by cunning
wiles. In Yung Chêng's reign the Hunanese Chang
Hsi and Tsêng Ching preached sedition against the
dynasty in their native province, while in Chia

Ch'ing's reign the palace conspiracy of Lin Ching dismayed that monarch in his capital. These events were followed by rebellions in Ssŭ-ch'uan and Shensi ; under Tao Kuang and his successor the T'ai-p'ings started their campaign from a remote Kuangsi village. Although these worthy causes were destined to ultimate defeat, the gradual trend of the national will became manifest. At last our own era dawned, the sun of freedom had risen, and a sense of the rights of the race animated men's minds. In addition the Manchu bandits could not even protect themselves. Powerful foes encroached upon the territory of China, and the dynasty parted with our sacred soil to enrich neighbouring nations. The Chinese race of to-day may be degenerate, but it is descended from mighty men of old. How should it endure that the spirits of the great dead should be insulted by the everlasting visitation of this scourge ?

" Then did patriots arise like a whirlwind, or like a cloud which is suddenly manifested in the firmament. They began with the Canton insurrection ; then Peking was alarmed by Wu Yüeh's bomb (1905). A year later Hsü Hsi-lin fired his bullet into the vitals of the Manchu robber-chief, En Ming, Governor of Anhui. Hsiung Chêng-chi raised the standard of liberty on the Yang-tsze's banks ; rising followed rising all over the empire, until the secret plot against the Regent was discovered, and the abortive

insurrection in Canton startled the capital. One
failure followed another, but other brave men took
the place of the heroes who died, and the empire
was born again to life. The bandit Manchu court
was shaken with pallid terror, until the cicada threw
off its shell in a glorious regeneration, and the present
crowning triumph was achieved. The patriotic
crusade started in Wu-ch'ang ; the four corners of
the empire responded to the call. Coast regions
nobly followed in their wake, and the Yang-tsze was
won back by our armies. The region south of the
Yellow River was lost to the Manchus, and the
north manifested its sympathy with our cause. An
earthquake shook the barbarian court of Peking,
and it was smitten with a paralysis. To-day it
has at last restored the government to the Chinese
people, and the five races of China may dwell together
in peace and mutual trust. Let us joyfully give
thanks. How could we have attained this measure
of victory had not your Majesty's soul in heaven
bestowed upon us your protecting influence ? I
have heard say that triumphs of Tartar savages over
our China were destined never to last longer than a
hundred years. But the reign of these Manchus
endured unto double, ay, unto treble, that period.
Yet Providence knows the appointed hour, and the
moment comes at last. We are initiating the
example to Eastern Asia of a republican form of

government ; success comes early or late to those who strive, but the good are surely rewarded in the end. Why then should we repine to-day that victory has tarried long ?

" I have heard that in the past many would-be deliverers of their country have ascended this lofty mound wherein is your sepulchre. It has served to them as a holy inspiration. As they looked down upon the surrounding rivers and upward to the hills, under an alien sway, they wept in the bitterness of their hearts, but to-day their sorrow is turned into joy. The spiritual influences of your grave at Nanking have come once more into their own. The dragon crouches in majesty as of old, and the tiger surveys his domain and his ancient capital. Everywhere a beautiful repose doth reign. Your legions line the approaches to the sepulchre ; a noble host stands expectant. Your people have come here to-day to inform your Majesty of the final victory. May this lofty shrine wherein you rest gain fresh lustre from to-day's event, and may your example inspire your descendants in the times which are to come. Spirit ! Accept this offering ! "

We are told by an eye-witness, Dr Lim Boon-keng, that when this ceremony was over, Sun Yat-sen turned to address the assembly. " He was speechless with emotion for a minute ; then he briefly declared how, after two hundred and sixty years, the nation had again recovered her freedom ; and now that the curse of Manchu domination was removed, the free peoples of a united republic could pursue their rightful aspirations. Three cheers for the president were now called for, and the appeal was responded to vigorously. The cheering was taken up by the crowds below, and then carried miles away by the thousands of troops, to mingle with the booming of distant guns."

LIST OF WORKS CONSULTED

The *I yü kuo chih* (costumes of strange nations). Circa 1380.

The *Tung hua lu* (a history of the Manchus down to A.D. 1735). 1765.

The *Shêng wu chi* (a history of the earlier wars under the Manchu dynasty). 1822.

A History of China, by REV. J. MACGOWAN, 1897.

A History of the Manchus, by REV. J. ROSS, 1880.

The Chinese Repository.

The Chinese and their Rebellions, by T. T. MEADOWS, 1856.

Pamphlets issued by the T'ai-p'ings, 1850-1864.

The Times, 1911-12.

The London and China Telegraph, 1911-12.

INDEX

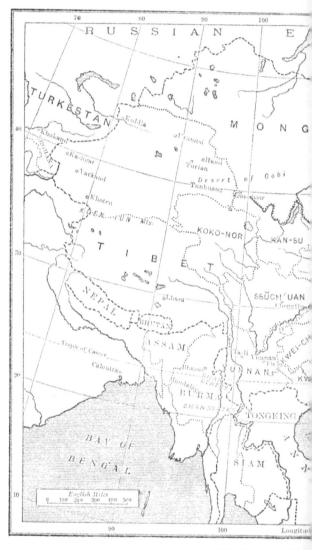

SKETCH MAP OF THE

www.ingramcontent.com/pod-product-compliance
Ingram Content Group UK Ltd.
Pitfield, Milton Keynes, MK11 3LW, UK
UKHW042145280225
455719UK00001B/113